A Workplace Survival Guide
For the Newbie

By Barry David

Copyright © 2014 by Barry David

Publisher: CreateSpace Independent Publishing Platform
ISBN-10: 1475026145
ISBN-13: 978-1475026146

My life is not my own. It was loaned to me to do great things with it. But I have strayed from the path that was laid before me. So from this day forth I promise to help others do great things with theirs. And in so doing, I just might repay my debt.

Barry David

Contents

Introduction

The workplace can be one of the most challenging ventures a young adult will face in his or her lifetime. Left unguided, a high percentage of new-comers find themselves in the black listed and soon to be terminated group. And trust me; this is one group that's easy to get in and very hard to get out. Survival, or the politically correct term longevity, depends on factors such as the individual's ability to learn quickly, develop credibility and network with the right people. And keep in mind that factors such as these should no longer be considered optional, but rather mandatory elements of achieving success in the work environment.

This book was written to aid the newbie, or anyone else in need of advice on how to survive in the workplace. And why such a harsh term as survival, well simply because it is so. A job will be one of the most significant activities that you will experience in your lifetime. You will spend more than half of your life doing it and almost everything you achieve will be because of it. Getting in is the easy part, it's the staying in that makes it difficult. And so hence the term, workplace survival.

No two work environments are the same, and the strategies to perform and excel are numerous. However, and no matter what the strategy the expected result should be the same, staying employed and potential advancement. Faced with this fact, the new employee will have to acquire the right knowledge and skills quickly in order to secure his or her continued employment.

This book will give you, the new or experienced employee a perspective of the work environment that is direct, simplified and honest. And as we go deeper, we will examine these factors as well as others and their impact on the employee.

The Interview- First Positive Impression.

Your interview is fast approaching and you are still indecisive as to what to wear, what to do and what to say. Everyone is telling you "hey you got this", but it really does not give you that reassuring feeling. And understandably so because this may be your very first job interview and you know that your chances of getting the job will depend on how you do in the interview.

Now the big day is finally here and you are sitting in front of the interviewer fully prepared for the interview. But ask yourself, are you really prepared for the interview? Probably not. And I'm not trying to be cynical; it's just that the interview can be a *one chance to get it right* kind of situation so you have to be sure that you are fully prepared.

Did you know that the interview session has become like any other test in which there is an interview format or test and resources (study material) to pass the test. You can buy books, watch videos and even search the web for material to help you pass an interview. And is there anything wrong with that? Of course not. If the passing of an interview was not a big deal, then I don't think that organizations would put time into creating prep articles, videos and guidance materials to help people improve their chances of success during an interview.

Although preparation for the interview is key, you should also be mindful that the interview itself is just part of the hiring process. And as a first time employee, you probably don't have a resume or at least one with stuff in it that can reference your skills and experience. However, you should not let it deter you because employers are often eager to take on the new untainted employee. But on that same note, don't get too cocky because there are some requirements that need to be met before you're in.

Have you ever heard the expression, first impression counts? Well if you haven't, it is an invaluable piece of information that you should know. And a positive first impression can be the deciding factor in you getting the job or you not.

So why is a positive first impression so important? Well besides the resume in your possession that your inexperience may render fruitless, your appearance, confidence, the way you speak and all other contributing factors to your level of professionalism will be key factors for nailing an interview. You probably do not wear a suit unless you're going to church or to a formal occasion such as a wedding. Probably, the last time you wore a suit was when you graduated high school or college. But hey, this is an interview and you want to look your best right? Well if you do, wearing a suit to your interview will provide the correct appearance for this event. So why a suit? A suit and office casual wear don't just make you look good, it shows that you have awareness and respect for the traditional norms of the interview and job hunting process. It is an overall part of making a good first impression. And it's not just your suit that's considered your wear. Jewelry, shoes, watches and belts are all part of your attire and you should proceed with caution when wearing these items. Basically, if it's too loud as in it can draw unnecessary attention and mistaken assumptions of you: don't wear it. And it's not just the wear; it's also the perfume, cologne and hairstyles both on your head and on your face. What you must do is ask yourself this question. Is what I'm wearing to the interview going to take away from who I am and guide the interviewers focus towards who I might be. Fancy beards and hairstyles, name belts, bright colored shoes, fancy watches, excessive and elaborate jewelry and strong perfume should always be avoided because these items can portray you in a negative. The best advice is to strive for simplicity. It is the individual, and what he or she can bring to the establishment that the interviewer is interested in anyway. What else you wear really does not matter as long as it is appropriate and you look presentable.

Now that we have covered the wear, you sit in the interview and do what, get interviewed? You answer questions and ask any that you may have at the end, right? Ok, maybe so, but consideration must be given for the way you answer the interview questions and the questions you want to ask. Some interview questions may be scenario based because the employer wants to evaluate how well you can assess and resolve problems. Other question may relate to matters that have nothing to do with the job itself. And as bizarre as some of these questions may seem they are used to evaluate something; and the answer is you. Even though some of your questions will evaluate your intellectual response, and some might be geared towards you physiological responses. It is still an evaluation of the individual. It is always you, the individual being evaluated.

The words you use, your tone and body language will all be used to evaluate you during the interview. Any of these qualities that give off a negative vibe can potentially harm the success of your interview. So in what manner do you approach these questions in order to be successful in the interview? The answer to that is, you adhere to a balanced level of self-confidence and professionalism during the interview process. Confidence and professionalism are two qualities that interviewers look for during your interview. Your ability to communicate/speak properly, confidently and in a professional manner will provide the best format for answering the interview questions. And how exactly does an individual speak properly? You speak properly by using the correct or appropriate words and tone during your conversation. In other words, avoid slang and speak politely. Words or speech described as slang, jargon, vernacular, lingo, argot, gobbledygook, you name it, should be avoided at all cost during the interview.

As part of the new generation, you are bombarded with words and phrases that impact you vocabulary. And as understandable as it may be that some of these words and phrases are not considered rude and or offensive, it is still not appropriate for conversation during an interview or any professional business matter. Your interviewer may not be familiar with the word usage or could even be offended by it. And rightly so, because slang and improper vocabulary has no place in the interview session.

So how do you avoid using these inappropriate words and phrases during the interview? You do so by practicing to do it correctly. Don't wait until the interview date to try and have a professional and appropriate conversation. Start practicing now. Practice is the only way to develop your professional communication skills. And with enough practice, you can switch you communication style on or off so you can communicate accordingly during any level of communication.

Your overall level of professionalism has a lot more to do with just the way you communicate. Your body language can be a significant indicator of the level of professionalism you have developed. An individuals' posterior as in the way they sit or stand, their facial expression, do they fold their arms and are they making eye contact can also be part of their interview evaluation. Slouching in a chair or sitting with your hands folded can give an impression of being bored or aggravated. Leaning against a wall, standing on one leg with one foot on the wall is definitely a sign of an individual who is lacking professionalism. Remember, you can be identified by an interviewer before the actual interview so be mindful of what you do even prior to the session. Maintaining eye contact is another important aspect of effective body language in relation to an interview. Not maintaining eye contact or looking away promotes a sense of insecurity, inferiority and guilt on your behalf. Your potential employer would like to know that the new hires exhibit the confidence to fill the position and establish themselves in the company. After all, would you hire someone who shows a lack of confidence or insecurity? Of course not, so why should someone hire you if you do not exhibit any confidence in yourself.

Having confidence is great but there is an old expression that states: too much of one thing is good for nothing. And as it relates to confidence, too much confidence can have a negative effect on your interview session. And the reason for that is if you exhibit too much confidence during the interview session you can be viewed as cocky.

And I can only assume that we all probably heard of cocky and understand its meaning. Well if you haven't it means arrogant. That overly confident person, that person that seems to know everything, does no wrong and has no problem telling you as it is, whenever and wherever. They may even give the interviewer the impression that they were the one being interviewed. Being overly confident only works against you and will lessen your chances of being picked for the position. Being mindful of when you can be viewed as arrogant is an important aspect of honing your balanced level of confidence and professionalism.

As mentioned before, the interview is a great opportunity to leave a first positive impression. Finding your balance of confidence and professionalism, coupled with the right attire and attitude will also help you in making that good first impression. And lastly, when you go for your interview, crack a smile. Let the interviewer know that you are happy to be there and happy for the opportunity to be interviewed for the position. You never can tell just how far your all-round positive approach to the interview can take you.

Training - Second Positive Impression

Just because you got the job and you're in the door, does it mean that everything is great in your world and you need not be concerned. Yes it's great and you are hired and training for the position but you still have to perform even if you are learning. The work related training is an important part of your employment, as it is a chance for you to be properly introduced into the company and most important; for you to learn what are the company's expectations of you.

Unless you have previous experience in the career field that you are working in, the orientation or training is a good time to get yourself acquainted with the field. You should also use this time to get acquainted with the company, its core values, the internal departments if applicable, and any resource that you may need in the future such as HR contacts, supplies, department leaders, supervisors, managers etc. Anyone or anything that would be valuable to you and aid you in completing your tasks successfully.

Most companies try to teach their new hires everything about the company and their expectations of the employee, and during the training they will achieve a considerable amount of it. But it's rather unlikely a company will be able to teach a new employee everything he or she needs to know about the company. However, they will in all likeliness try to cover the most important aspects of the new employees role, the companies way of doing things and the pertinent rules and regulations as it pertains to the new hire. And in knowing this, it is important for every new employee to try and take away as much as possible from the training; to ensure that they are well prepared to meet the expectations, and perform in the manner that the company expects that they should.

So how do you measure performance in a training environment one might ask? Well besides any physical or knowledge based testing that may also be performance standards during your training, there are other factors that contribute to your performance. Taking notes, asking questions, volunteering and interacting during scenarios are some of the ways that you can add further recognition to your performance. Simply taking notes can help you gain some positive recognition, especially when the instructor advises the class to do so. Taking notes will also help you to retain vital information that you may forget, due to the sheer volume of information you have to take in during your training. You will also have a point of reference to go to if you need to remember something or reference something later on in your employment. Point to note however, don't hold back the class by taking too long to jot down your notes. Write as quickly and as accurately as possible and if you miss anything, you should try to follow up with the lecturer at the end of the class or during a break.

Asking questions is one of the most fundamental ways to verify interaction and show interest in what is being taught. The quality and the quantity of your questions go a long way as well. For example, it will be hard to describe asking only one question or being called-out to answer a question as involvement or interaction in a training environment. You have to ask questions and sensible ones as well, for it to count as involvement and interaction.

Now there is no standard number of questions to ask during training that would qualify as noticeable interaction, however, a healthy amount of quality or sensible questions will certainly be more productive to the session, rather than a whole lot of useless ones. And even if you heard the term "there is no such thing as a stupid question", don't take that statement to literal. My friend, there is such a thing as a stupid question and as an instructor I have heard countless numbers of them. The only truth is most instructors will maintain a professional standard and not point out the uselessness of the questions but rather redirect or restructure the question to make it relevant to the training. Now by all means this is recognition but definitely not the kind that you want. So when asking questions, try to ensure that they are relevant to the training, beneficial to the class, sensible and if not related to the training at least useful to all. And one final note on the question communication aspect of interacting during training. Never become confrontational with an instructor or another trainee. Even if you know that you are 100% correct it would be best to confirm your results in a one on one forum, rather than the whole class of attendees. Choosing to resolve the discrepancy in a controlled one on one setting shows a high level of professionalism and integrity, and will be greatly appreciated by the person receiving the correction to their error.

As the training is going along, the instructor asks for a volunteer to come up and assist with a scenario. Oh boy, you feel that tingling feeling in your stomach that lets you know it's time to be as inconspicuous as possible. Limiting any sort of acknowledgment of your existence. In your head you have already told the trainer don't even think about it buddy. If you, Mr. Trainer value your life, you will fix your gaze somewhere else in this room and dear not entertain the thought of choosing me. Me up there, me a willing volunteering, NEVER in this lifetime. Nothing can be as uncomfortable as standing, speaking and interacting in front of a group of people and trust me, I have been there. But if you are able to get over this fear you will be able to tap into further possibilities for making a good impression on the instructor.

If you still have the jitters of standing in front of a group then you could be losing out on some potential positive recognition. And you not only gain recognition from the instructor but also your future peers. One of the greatest signs of confidence is an individual's ability to perform and or speak in front of a crowd. But please keep in mind that you are not seeking an award for best performing actor so keep it proper. Remember there are impressions that you may not want to leave with the instructor and the rest of the attendees, so be on your best behavior and keep it professional and only casual or entertaining when permissible. But don't worry; the instructors will create the environment that warrants the applicable behavior so all you have to do is follow his or her lead.

But why is all of this interacting necessary and how does it equate to a performance that can be measured? Well in case you did not know, many company lecturers and instructors are actual employees, and some of them even hold top management positions in the company. For instance the CEO, Director or Safety manager may actually be the folks teaching the class and as mentioned before, this is a great opportunity to make a second positive impression. Imagine how positive and promising your career can be if during your training, you were able to gain some form of recognition with top management and other leadership members based on your in class performance.

And I can tell you from experience of being a manager and a class instructor that I have come across people who have made lasting impressions on me during the training. At the end of the training, the other instructors and I would discuss officially and at times casually, the performance of the new hires and who we see as potential candidates with successful career paths. I have even had the pleasure of seeing some of them move up in the company and whenever I see these individuals, I often remind them of their positive performance during the training class for which they are often very pleased to hear about.

So if your new job has a training session as part of the hiring process, you should use this opportunity to make a positive impression on your future peers and possibly one of your managers or supervisors, who may very well be one of the lecturers. Remember to ask relevant questions, interact professionally, volunteer and take notes to ensure you have a future reference you can go back to when needed. And finally, avoid instances of confrontational or argumentative communication. Take in as much as you can, leave only a positive impression.

Probation- Third Positive Impression, First Real Evaluation

The probation is another critical junction point in your employment. And you should be just as cautious and working at your best, as you did when you first interviewed and trained for the job. Your probation period is a part of your employment that creates a buffer for your employer to evaluate your performance at actually doing the job. In addition, your employer can ultimately make the decision if they should keep you or not. In other words, if you are not a got fit or better yet not working out as expected you can be terminated. And termination is never a good thing. Even if you hear someone say "I'm glad they fired me", trust me when I say that nothing can be further from the truth. So it's important to remember that even though you are an employee of the company and you receive pay and benefits, you can still be dismissed for poor performance at any time during this period.

As you start working and the longer you work, you can easily become complacent and experience traits of poor performance standards. This is why it is absolutely important for new employees to stay on point, meaning stay focused and maintain awareness of their performance standards. In some institutions there is also an evaluation of your performance during your probation, which can lead to a pay increase or not, depending on where your performance standards measure up to. So if you want to maximize on every financial increase and start the process of excelling in your career, then ensure that you put your best foot forward and maintain a professional work standard - Always, no exceptions.

Most people who are enthusiastic about their job or in any other way enjoy doing their job. Can usually find ways to maneuver around bouts of complacency. And the folks who become complacent are usually the ones who have lost their enthusiasm about the job, or doing their job, and do not definitively seek ways of finding solutions. So how did they get to this point? Their resentment towards their job, the people at work or the institution or a combination of any of these factors can easily become the fuel for their performance. Complacency in workers is usually borne of negative situations such as harboring on a poor experience, not being able to complete their tasks and assignments in the expected manner, not accepting of the rules, regulations, P&P's or simply the companies' way of doing things. In addition, this list can include unfair work practices by supervisors and managers, lack of support from management, misinformation and not feeling appreciated.

It is important to keep in mind that although the institution can be the source of an employee's grievance and reason for their complacent demeanor, the same applies to the individual who may be culpable for their state of unhappiness through their own doing. For example, being suspended for tardiness is simply being suspended for arriving to work late. No matter what your reason is for arriving to work late, and hopefully it's not because of some inane reason such as you don't like being at work or you can't stand your boss: because it makes no difference. The suspension can be considered a poor experience by the employee because they may have felt that their tardiness was justifiable, or the supervisor could have been a bit more understanding. However, this grievance has nothing to do with the company and the resolve to this poor performance is totally in the hands of the employee. This is why it is very important for you to not take someone else's grievances or poor experience as your own. Or give it leverage to any poor experience you may have had yourself. I mention this now because it is something that you will be exposed to in the workplace, and it can be very tempting to be considerate of your peer's grievances even to the point of acting on it. In a later chapter, we will discuss negative experiences of both you and your peers but for now I urge you to never use the experiences of others, especially if you do not know both sides of the story.

So far, your probationary period seems like nothing but a system to get rid of you by capitalizing on your mistakes but nothing could be further from the truth. In fact, the probationary period is actually a system that works in your favor and gives a certain degree of leniency based on the fact that you can make mistakes and you are still learning. And if you play your cards right, you can also use this period of employment to gain valuable recognition and leave a third positive impression.

So just how does one play their cards right? And if you are not familiar with the term, it means doing everything necessary to win or succeed. Doing your job as the company expects you too or by-the-book is a good start. Also, avoiding the temptation to take short-cuts from any process is key during your probationary period. Adopting this standard will be very helpful if you ever mess up and something goes wrong during the performance of your duty.

Whenever we mess up, the company will perform an investigation to get to the bottom of the issue. They will look at the evidence wherever applicable and the results of the error. Upon completion of the investigation, the company will make a decision based on their findings. And in most cases the company tends to mainly take into consideration, what caused the error as opposed to the error itself. Leading to the final decision not based as a result of the issue, (as in you crashed the vehicle) but often because of the events that led up to it (what were you doing that resulted in the car crash). Now there are certainly standards where for example a collision due to no fault or at fault can lead to dismissal, and you should make every effort to avoid significant errors when at work. My example however, is based on scenarios where the degree of punitive measures is decided based on more than a standardized process for dealing with job related infringements. And to further explain, you may crash the vehicle, but you being cautious and making a mistake can yield a different result to you being reckless and negligent while operating the vehicle.

So here is where we look at errors and the two most significant factors as it relates to you having one during your probationary period. There is the error in process and error by omission or change. In an error in process, you did everything by the book but an incident occurred anyway. In the error by omission or change, you didn't do everything by the book because a part of the process was not completed or you changed part of the process resulting in the error. As a manager, whenever I investigated an employee related matter I would not only look at the resulting issue, but more so what led up to the issue. If the employee made a mistake because they followed the process and the error was due to his or her inexperience, I would probably assign a lesser punitive measure than compared to an employee making a mistake because he or she did things their own way. Or purposely omitted part of the process. Now make no mistake, when you mess up that's your mistake even if you followed the process to the tee. But messing up in this manner may grant you some degree of clemency and a second chance as compared to messing up any other way. Point to note, this does not mean that you can take it easy and not be on your guard against errors just because there is a huge possibility that you can make good on a bad situation. It simply means that if you do end up making a mistake, let it be within the job specific guidelines so your chances of recovery is best.

Your probation if you have one is your opportunity to make a third positive impression and prove your metal in your first real evaluation. But as you can see, there are also possibilities for you to have bad experiences that can jeopardize your employment. But never fear, mistakes can and will happen, but the important thing to know is you must own up to it, learn from it and try not to repeat it. In time, some of your earlier mistakes can even be removed from your file and may not count against advancement opportunities. But to be absolutely safe, the best approach is to not have any issues or make any major mistakes at all. In a later chapter we will speak more on work related mistakes and how an individual can avoid and or recover from them.

Finally, besides avoiding work related errors, there are certain aspects of your probation that must be adhered to. Performing at you best, maintaining a professional standard, minimizing absences and lateness and going above and beyond your task to contribute to the establishment and your team, are some of the necessary standards you should adopt. And you should try to do so as quickly as possible. When you do, you will not only be able to hammer down a positive impression, but you will also be able to achieve a positive first real work evaluation.

New Kid On The Block

Yes you are definitely one of the people within the organization and good for you. You're probably still under probation or recently completed it. But nevertheless, you're in. And it's great to be in. But you are still the newbie and you are still learning as you go along. And you should always be on full alert and maintain awareness of the things that can hurt your career.

Even if you have some experience or if this is your first rodeo in the work environment, you should proceed with caution because the things that you do can determine the type of environment you create. I have had different jobs and one thing remains the same, it's always harder to get in than to get out. And it's often easier to fail than it is to succeed. The process to get a job can at times be extensive and may incur personal expenses, so I try my best not to waste my time and money due to situations I more than likely had control over. The workplace arena, and yes arena is a highly competitive environment and a new employee who does not possess the right knowledge and skill to retain their employment, can be in and out in a blink of an eye.

So how does one gain the knowledge and skills necessary to survive in the workplace arena? You do so by developing good office politics, learning quickly, being able to adapt to new situations expeditiously and structuring your work performance and standards around the company core values and expectations of you. In later chapters we will discuss these attributes but for now, let's focus on what to expect from the people who work in the organization and how to deal with what they teach you or influences you are exposed too.

From the first day, your first exposure to the work environment will be guidance, advice and maybe some criticism. The amount you receive will also share an opposite equivalency to the amount of experience you possess. In essence, more experience less advice and criticism, no experience a whole lot of it. So at this point please proceed with caution when it comes to guidance, advice and what you may perceive as constructive criticism. Not all will be good or in your best interest so apply your mental resourcefulness of investigating, analyzing and deducing before applying anything learned. Some of it can be so straightforward that you need not put thought into it and immediately disregarded. Some however, can be very deceptive and may seem useful and harmless. It's this type of advice and guidance that does the most damage to a new employee's career. And although your wrongdoing may be as a result of deceit, it may not be enough to save your job or remove any negative perception of you.

To avoid finding yourself in situations like these, you have to be able to validate the information and advice you receive. As mentioned earlier, some of it can be dismissed as corruptive, but how do you validate the ones not so easy to decipher? This step requires a somewhat delicate process because not only do you want to validate the info, you don't want to offend the person who gave you the advice or guidance. One good way to validate information and guidance is to speak to a supervisor, manager or someone considered as a senior respectable employee. And why such an individual, because they are employees who give advice based on the companies rules, policies and standards. After all, I don't think any of these folks will want someone to say that they told them to do the wrong thing. So speak to them about anything work related and I repeat work related, that you need a second opinion on.

Now that you have that part covered, how do you not offend the person that you worked with? Well what you have to do is simply omit any name or reference to person place or thing. Present your information from a first person point of view. For example don't say "I was made to understand that we can use the supervisors as a reference". Instead you should say, "Can I use the supervisor as a reference".

Another work related setting you will be exposed to is attitude. Some positive, some negative and some that will drive you up a wall. But when we talk about attitude what do we mean? Well it's the body language, tone and words used by an individual to convey an inappropriate or demeaning message that invokes disregard of another. And unfortunately, as the new kid on the block you may experience a lot of it so be prepared. The positive and negative attitudes that your coworkers or bosses will bring to the work environment is not necessarily your fault, but it is something you have to deal with during your employment. And in dealing with them I mean working in the attitude setting and not fixing it, because I do not believe that an employee's or bosses disruptive attitude is yours to fix. At least not for the moment. Probably later on when you stand on the top of the totem pole and your ID says BOSS, then you can fix it. But for now, let's work on dealing with the attitude. In my experience, the best way to deal with attitude is not to return it. A mature and professional approach to conflicts arisen from someone's attitude will work in your favor, especially as a new employee. At times the best response is none, except if it's your boss and your silence can be viewed as disrespect. And if it is your boss, keep it on a mature level, professional and keep it short. I have witnessed situations where the innocent party, through anger conducted themselves in a disruptive manner and in turn, received a harsher penalty for the incident. Or even worse, receive the only penalty and the instigating party walked away scotch free. Your ability to remain professional, and hold your reserve in the presence of your peers and bosses when dealing with conflicts will do great justice to your character. In later chapters we will discuss how to go about avoiding conflicts and dealing with them when avoidance is unavoidable.

Yes it can be difficult and often intimidating being the new kid on the block. But don't let it get to you. And never let your fear or intimidation be a guiding factor in your decision making. You are new, you are not without resourcefulness. As long as you know who to turn to and what advice, guidance and criticism is in your best interest; your time as a newbie can be joyous and without incident.

Is This Job Right For Me?

By now you should know right? But it's never that easy. Sometimes a job can seem to be perfect and later on you develop concerns over whether you should stay or go. Sometimes it's the opposite and you start off not wanting to stay, but later on, you have a change of heart and decide to stick it through. But before you can make a final determination on if you should stay or go, there is one question that you must answer. And this is the question: is it the job or is it me? Is there something with the job that's causing me to not to want to be here anymore or is it me? Am I the reason why the job has become unbearable? What a silly question. Of course it's the job and it can only be the job. There is no way it could be me.

There are times when the Job is not for you and you absolutely know it. For example, you are an ER tech and on your first day at work you see a dead body. The sight of a dead body make you nauseous, sick, light-headed and you eventually collapse to the floor. You try to shake it off and give it another shot. It was your first experience and it was an intense moment for you. About a half an hour later, a disemboweled patient comes into the ER. And if you are not familiar with the term disemboweled, it means the person's guts hanging out of their stomach. The sight of this sickens you so much that you can't even keep your eyes open long enough to assist the doctor. Everyone is looking at you and calling out to you to open your eyes and pay attention. But you are deadlocked in a trance, trying to take your mind off of what you just saw. With the folks continuously calling on you to help, you decide in that moment that you need to face your fears. You open your eyes just

29

long enough to witness the doctor holding the patient's intestines and replacing it into his stomach. Everything goes black and with that, it's another lights out for you. The ER staff now has two patients to worry about.

I'm sure by now we can both agree that clearly, this job is not for you and you moving on would be totally understandable. And I'm sure that your coworkers would definitely appreciate you having the guts "no pun intended" to move on. But situations like the one just mentioned are usually the exception and not the rule when it comes to a lack of job satisfaction, or at minimum, job contentment. You would probably know that being an exterminator and having a terrible fear of insects, won't work very well as far as a career of choice. Or even better, you sign up for a sky diver instructor course and cannot even stand at the top of a ten foot ladder and look down.

For the most part, a job would not be right for the individual because of the individual and not necessarily the job itself. Take for example the job of a taxi driver. At any time in a major metropolitan city, there are hundreds of taxis and taxi drivers on the streets. The job of a taxi driver is to take passengers from point A to point B. Factors associated with the job of a taxi driver include: maintaining professionalism, safety awareness, situational awareness, safe driving, customer relations, problem solving, conflict resolution, multitasking, constant vigilance and critical thinking just to name a few. Most of the drivers have either grown to like their job or accept their job. Some decide that the job is not right for them and they move on. The ones that move on usually do so because of either the job itself, or the factors associated with the job.

But wait. Based on what I just said, it seem like there is a higher probability that it could be the job and not so much the individual as the primary cause for wanting to leave. And it seems fair enough because there are many factors of the job that can be so negative; it can cause an employee to want to leave. But nothing could be further from the truth. Most of the time it's not the situation itself, but rather the individual in the situation. It's the individual's level of professional standard and ability to deal with these negative factors that make the difference.

For example, a certain pet store has a very unmanageable dog that drives the workers crazy. On the night shift, one of the workers put the dog outside in the cold so he would not hear the dog barking. Other workers just try to ignore the barking, while others try to find ways to calm the dog down so it will not bark. The barking dog is a factor of the job. How the situation is dealt with is on the individual. People will always blame the job or the people at work or the factors related to the job as a reason for not wanting to be part of the company. But for every one that can't do it there is ten, twenty or even a hundred who can. So never get in the habit of blaming a job or the factors associated with the job for you reason of not being satisfied or happy with the job. Identify what the underlying issue is and work at fixing it on your end, before you come to your conclusion that the job is not right for you. We have a lot more control over the job and factors related to the job than we give ourselves credit for. I have often seen employees totally give up on their job and blaming the job for them not wanting to do it anymore. Now I'm not saying that there aren't situations that will be of concern to the point where the employee should part ways. In fact there are. And not every problem is solvable. And if you ever encounter such a situation you should do what you think is right. Trying to make it work might actually be a bad thing, but this is something you will have to figure out and decide.

The key point here is to evaluate, try to fix it and if not, then make your decision to move on. In the end, you will have to know what's right for you. But it will be in your best interest to always give it a fair chance to see if it is salvageable before you decide to move on. And if you don't part ways the right way, you may not be able to come back so always leave in a respectable manner. The job you left could very well end up being a better place than where you're at. So never close doors behind you because you never know if you may need to come back in.

I Hate This Job - Ok Pause For A Second. This Is Serious

Sometimes we despise a job so much that we lose all sense of professionalism. This is a mental place that no employee should ever get too. As an employee, you should also be aware of the signs of impending doom. And why doom, because an employee you compromises his or her integrity can end up doing stuff that they can come to regret. Sometimes what they end up doing can be so egregious, that they subject themselves to termination, external investigation and legal mitigation up to fines and even worse, incarceration.

It is very important for an employee to realize when he or she is approaching a point of actually hating their job. When you are aware that you are highly unsatisfied with your job, you can take action to ensure that you do not take on a work demeanor that invites poor conduct and performance. Remember in the past chapter we used an example of a pet store employee, putting a dog outside in the cold so he would not have to deal with hearing the dog bark. His resolve to the problem is outright inhumane and can even be considered as animal abuse. This young man could have gotten so upset that he put aside any sense of morality, just so he could have an easier time at work. And it can get even worse when this behavior becomes a part of his normal routine, and he believes that he has found a way to adjust or solve the problem. Now he may have adjusted, but did he truly find a solution or solved the problem?

In the workplace, a true solution does not only benefit one person. It benefit's all. You, the people at work, the company and its vision. And if it's a good idea you should not have a problem sharing it with others right? I highly doubt that this employee would go tell his manager that he found a way to quiet the noisy dog. And of course not, because he knows that his actions would be totally unacceptable and he might even lose his job.

So what contributes to this type of behavior? What can cause an employee to hate the job so much that they resort to using inappropriate behavior, as a means of dealing with issues at the job? Frankly, there are many factors. However, we can associate almost any issue with three major components of the job. And these three categories are: the job itself or the system, the people, and finally factors related to the job. Keep in mind that "system" is a vague expression that also encompasses format, procedure, rules, policies etc., as it relates to the job, or any job specific format for completing your tasks. People will consist of coworkers, bosses, customers, clients etc. And factors relate to anything applicable to you performing your duties such as client behavior, weather conditions, multitasking, problem solving, conflict resolution, you name it. If it applies and in some way affects your work, then it's a factor.

If we go back to the taxi driver and his or her job is to transport passengers in a non-interactive driver-client environment down a straight or uncomplicated route, the driver would more or less be ok with the job, happy with it, or bored to the point of wanting to leave. The job itself is not necessarily the issue. But when we add the people, the supervisors, dispatchers, the other drivers on the road and of course the traffic; we increase the responsible actions of the driver. Now let's add the system which is the way or the expected manner the driver should complete his or her task. Take this route, avoid that route, drive safely, give out a business card or flyer, assist the passengers with luggage etc. And finally, let's add the applicable factors. Passengers taking their time, dispatched to a far pickup, impolite supervisor, impolite passengers, issue with collecting payment from passengers, passengers being rude and condescending, and the lists goes on. Any one of these or combination of these factors can make an employee feel hate for their job. And when it becomes overbearing, they can either act out on it in a disruptive manner, or find ways to mitigate the issue that are not appropriate to the work environment. As in the case of the pet store worker who in an effort to resolve the issue, left the dog outside in the cold. But of issues related to people, the job or system and the applicable factors, which one do you think takes the hardest toll on an employee? Well if you choose the people you are one 100% correct.

For the most part, the average person can overcome any hard feelings with the job or the system and the factors. Especially the external factors or the ones that change depending on the circumstance, such as a rude customer. But when it comes to people. It's way harder to get over. That's because the people give the issue a sense of winning and losing. It becomes personal when you throw in the stomach aching and nerve swelling poisonous ingredients such as attitude, tone and sarcasm you may also receive from them. It's on baby. This is not going to go away anytime soon. This is now a life crisis where only your departure from the company or theirs, will bring this conflict to an end. This is why as true professionals we should never take things personal. Way easier said than done but I guarantee if you can master it, you will ascend at lightning speed to becoming a Zen master in the art of professionalism. In later chapters we will discuss not taking things personal in more detail but for now we will stay focused on the effects of people, systems and factors on your job, and your mentality towards it.

Second would be the system. This can be very difficult and frustrating for an employee, especially when they cannot get guidance from someone in order to eliminate the problem. If we're just not getting it or coming up short on tasks, we can often resort to saying stuff like "the job is too hard" or "they ask you to do so much around here". Realistically, I don't believe the company would knowingly ask the employees to do something that they cannot deliver on. And to my readers who have had their company ask them to do one thousand things beyond the comprehension, skills and abilities of humans, remember I said "knowingly". Pushing employees to do more is something that companies often do in an effort to get more bang for their buck. Which means, try to get more out of the employee. If you're not getting it or coming up short then it's mostly on you. I'm sure there are other people in the company who are able to complete their tasks and assignments. Often enough, if we put our best foot forward and put some thought into it (you know, effort), we can almost always overcome these obstacles. Having patience and developing experience will go a long way in helping you to overcome these obstacles as it relates to your tasks and the way you ought to complete them. Patience and experience will also help you to overcome the applicable factors that are linked to the job. As time goes by and you develop experience, your tasks will become easier and you will be able to deal with the issues within the system that made your job difficult.

Lastly we look at factors. And although there may be similarity between the system and the factors, we make a distinction because the factors can have high variation and be inconsistent, whereas the system is structured with little or no variation at all. The applicable factors can also make the job seem more difficult than it really is. However, it's the part that's probably the easiest to deal with or get over. And this is because the factors can be intermittent and usually will not repeat itself in its entirety. For example, I got into a small car accident and the driver of the other vehicle was yelling and screaming at me. Chances are you will not get into an accident every day (unless you are a really horrible driver) and at some time you will get over the incident. It's also the part that we take less personal and can make a faster recovery. It's the rude passenger that we just so happen to pick up today. Yeah it got to you but you probably won't see that passenger again and soon after, you forget about it and let it go. However, it can become bothersome when it maintains as part of the daily routine. For example; there is a rude passenger that you transport daily or the dispatcher with the bad attitude works on all of your shifts so they become part of your daily routine. When this happens, we give it foundation as part of the system and the people associated with the job. Now I hate my job because of the very rude passenger I have to transport every day, or I hate my job because of the nasty and rude speaking dispatcher that works my shifts during the week. The truth is you hate the passenger and the dispatcher because of their attitude and not the job. But ultimately, the job will suffer for it. You should always try to put things in perspective so you can minimize the mental energy and focus you use to deal with it. Getting ferociously upset because of a rowdy person and having a bad day at work, is something you do not have to do. You have a choice. Do you think that the rude passenger is thinking about you after he or she leaves the cab or their interaction with you is going to ruin their day? Do you think that the dispatcher will have a bad day after being rude to you? Probably not. So why should you. You have control over your emotional response and as a professional, this is a skill you will have to hone in order to deal with behaviors and personalities that pry at your professionalism and composure. The last thing you should be doing is falsely blaming the job for your dissatisfaction, because you did not identify the true cause of your issue or issues. So before you start believing that this job is the worst thing that ever happened to you. You should ask yourself, is it the job or is it me? Is it the people, my tasks or the way things should be done, or is it the applicable factors associated with this job that makes me hate my job? I think that after making a strong evaluation of the issue or issues and looking at ways to solve them, there just may be a positive outlook in the end. And remember you should never get to a point of hate that you resort to doing something that will get you in trouble. Maintain you professionalism and if it comes to the worst, move on respectfully.

So we know what can make us hate our job but is there anything we can do to get us back to liking our job? Of course there is and it's very simple too. What you will have to do is work on the obstacles that make you feel upset about your job and can go as far as preventing you from going into work. You should focus on the aspect of your job or the people who make it better, when you don't feel like being there. It can be a coworker, supervisor or even the customer that you have a good relationship with. It can be driving, seeing new places or interacting with new people. A favorite task or assignment that makes you feel fulfilled and enjoy that part of your job, could also be the reason that make you go into work. No matter what it is, when you find it, work on it. Make it your motivation to keep doing what you do until you find other ways to deal with the issues your experiencing. Maintaining a positive outlook will always do more in helping you to find a solution to the problem, than a negative one.

The Job

If you're a carpenter, then your job may be to build furniture or cabinets. If you're a pro athlete, then your job is to play a sport and potentially win games. After all, what good is a carpenter who can't build stuff, or an athlete who cannot play to win games?

When it comes to the job, most people look at issues that relate to themselves, which is typically their own task and assignments that they need to complete. I come to work, complete my tasks and assignments and then I leave. I am also very good at what I do so my work day is a breeze. But there is a distinction between "Your Job" and "The Job" and it's very important to know it, and work towards satisfying both aspects of it.

To further explain, we will use an example of a security officer working for a large department store. So you are the security officer working for a large department store and part of your core function is to prevent or minimize theft. The other part of your job is to provide a safe shopping experience for the customers. You work from 9am-5pm and your performance is great. However, on one particular day your relief did not show up and your supervisor asked if you could stay to cover the shift because she was a bit short on staff. You politely refused because you were looking forward to getting off on time to simply enjoy some you-time. The next day, you found out that the store was robbed of $2000 worth of items and this was due to the fact that there was not enough security staffing at the time.

Now in no way shape or form is this loss to the department store your fault. You did your job. But what about your company? Did your company do its job?

Everything that we do as employees is part of a bigger task or responsibility of the company. And just because an individual does his or her job it does not correlate to the company accurately or completely doing its job. So of more importance than the individual doing his or her job, is the individual working to ensure that the company does its job and fulfill its obligation to its customers and clients. For most employees, self-achievement or self-gain is the main motivator for working or even working harder. But this does not equate to success because true success is a result that you, your coworkers, the institution and even the clients and customers can benefit from. Individual achievement is great but does not contribute to positives such as company sustainability, job security, company and employee growth and development.

In John F. Kennedy's Inaugural Address of January 20, 1961, his statement "ask not what your country can do for you — ask what you can do for your country" bears resemblance to the fact that the ultimate success lies in the contributions of the people for the betterment of the business. Just as the success of the country weighs on the contributions of its citizens. If we look at the institution as an individual and align our efforts towards the satisfactory completion of the institutions tasks and assignments and not just our own, then we are truly aligned with our organizational obligations.

Adherence To Company Values

The company's' values is the fundamental beliefs and aspirations of the company. It is the standard by which the company tries to set for itself both explicitly and implicitly. And this standard is displayed to all involved which includes the people who work for the company and the customers and clients. So why should I being a new employee, adhere to the company's values and of what benefit is it to me? Well adherence to the company values confirms your understanding and acceptance of its vision and your loyalty to the mission.

Have you ever heard the term "a company man"? Well it's a generic term that describes an individual who does things by the book or for some, an individual who sees things from the companies' perspective. This individual can also receive a negative or positive outlook from his or her peers on their classification of being a company man. For example, if an employee has something negative to say about the company and the pro-company individual speaks in favor of it, then he or she can be seen in a negative light. On the same token, someone may need advice on how to properly do a procedure or deal with an issue and now pro-company person becomes a positive light because of their knowledge of the proper processes, or doing things by the book. But this chapter is not about the negative or positive outcome linked to adherence to the core values of a company. It is about "why" the individual should adhere.

Well to be blunt and first and foremost, it is part of your job. And it's also part of your expectations set by your employer. Doing your job in accordance to the company's core values is how the company expects you to do the job. Every action you take should be guided by the company's core values. And for example, let's say that one of the company's core values is based on safety. And if I were to be more specific, it's based on driver safety because you are a cabdriver working for a cab company. This means that during your day, the way you drive should always be aligned with the company's core value of safety first. And you should not approach your driving responsibilities in any other way. Now I'm sure that everyone should adopt safe driving habit's whether is a job or not, and establishing a company core value on driving safety may seem unnecessary. After all, who wants to get in an accident and cause harm to themselves or others? The purpose of establishing the core value is to build the company around an ideal of safety first. And to help ensure that all employees, customers and clients, are aware of the companies' position on safe driving practices.

So this is why you are encouraged to adhere to the core values of the company. Because it is what gives the company its identity and helps set its standard. Adherence is also important because not only does it show that you are as they say - playing by the rules; it also keeps you in the safe zone. Whenever something goes wrong, the first thing the employer looks at is if the employee was doing things the way it should've been done. Being known for doing things in a mirrored fashion to the core values of the company, will go a long way in giving your side of the story some validity. Now it will not remove any wrong doing on its own. But in instances where the verdict can go for or against you, having some credibility on your performance as it relates to you working in cohesion with the core values of the company will definitely help to tip the scale in your favor. Especially in situations where the evidence is not clearly in your favor.

I remember an incident when I was accused by a client for not providing an acceptable level of customer service. I received a call from my boss that I was being investigated, and he wanted to know what happened and get my side of the story. I explained to my boss exactly what had happened, so he told me that he will look into the matter some more and get back to me. Now to give you some insight into the situation, this was an interaction between me and a client so in this kind of situation you basically have a stale mate. My word against hers with no substantial evidence to prove either of us right or wrong.

So as part of the investigation, my boss spoke to my immediate supervisor about me and what kind of person she knew me to be. She had nothing but favorable words to describe my character. And above all else she reinforced my side of the story with my known adherence to going about my tasks in the way the organization expects of me. By being known for following the rules and doing my job in the expected manner, I was able to tip the scale in my favor. The investigation concluded that I was not at fault and in the end, no further issues arose from it. And just in case you were wondering, my supervisor vouching for me had nothing to do with the length of time I had been at the company just in case you were wondering. I was still very new to the company. My performance and work standards were enough for my supervisor to believe my side of the story.

Understanding the core values, and knowing how it relates to your tasks and expectations is very important to your career and success.

It is a value system that should be engrained in every employee and expressed through their every action because the company's success depends on it. And this is no secret because the company will and understandably do, whatever is necessary to ensure that employees adhere to the core values in an effort to maintain its standard. By adopting these standards early in your employment, it will certainly help both you and the institution on your pathway to success.

What Else Is Expected Of Me? My Organizational Obligation

I remember when I was a young eager employee, with charm and personality that seemed immeasurable. I could talk the talk and walk the walk. I was a star employee with sound work ethics and I was highly ambitious. Always early for work, stayed back to help out and did not ask for much. The perfect employee right?

Well not exactly. I had one problem that I did not realize until it was explained to me that it was a problem. You see, I had no problem in exercising my right to use the time off that I had. If I was sick or had an out of work related issue, I would simply take the day off instead of resolving the ailment or issue and going to work. And why should I? I had the time right? Well that's what I though and I never saw it as an issue. However, that's not what my (OC) officer-in-charge taught and we eventually had a conversation about what he would refer to as my excessive absences. But before we get to the conversation, I will tell you about the events that led up to it.

It all began with a small misunderstanding. As most issues do. And I always thought that because I had great punctuality and went the extra mile, I was in my CO's good graces. And as an employee, who always arrives early for work, I was always able to negotiate my daily assignments and my CO was always accommodating. But not on this day, the day I learned and understood the meaning of my organizational obligation in relation to my job, employer and coworkers. You see, my equal opposite nemesis was a guy we will call Larry. Larry was everything I'm not. Always late, charmless and just did his job. But Larry always walked around with a smile on his face and a worry free demeanor. It puzzled me that he was always late but never seemed to be penalized. So on my day of awakening, which happened to be the day I came in late and was not able to choose my assignment, because you know who finally came in early and got it. You guessed it, Larry. I asked my CO if he could change the assignments and he said no. When my charm did not work I resorted to making demands for which I taught was justifiable, especially coming from a self-proclaimed "model employee".

That's when my CO taught me the importance of my responsibility to the workplace. I was told that although my punctuality and willingness to help out were admirable traits, it becomes meaningless if I am not at work. He said we are in the business of people being here, and you not being here is bad for business. He further went on to say that for as long as I have known him (Larry) he has never taken a day off for being sick or out of work issue. In fact, he also covers a lot of the shifts that you and your fellow coworkers call out for. He (Larry) gives me late, you give me absent - I can work with late but not absent. So much for me being that great employee.

So what exactly is my organizational obligation? Well it's simply my level of commitment to the overall maintenance and development of me, my coworkers and the institution. A high level of commitment to their coworkers and the company is a significant trait that an employee can possess. That drive that compels you to go in to work even if you're not one hundred percent or to offer to cover a shift even if you made prior arrangements is a most admirable characteristic amongst your peers and bosses. Remember, every time you don't come in someone else will have to do your tasks and it can be harder for them if their just coming off theirs. Also, consideration should be given to the fact that the individual covering your tour may have made arrangements themselves. Suppose they had an emergency or a much needed appointment to attend to. How would you feel if that were you? Now in no way am I saying that if you are genuinely sick or have a serious emergency, you should neglect these situations and go into work. What you have to do is make a concerted effort to try and make it to work. Don't just say well I'm sick and I have the time. You should exhaust every possibility that will enable you to go into work before calling out sick. But that's not all and your organizational obligation goes beyond not going into work. When you supervisor asks you to work a couple more hours to complete a project or participate by providing input to improve your operations, it is also part of your organizational obligation.

Acknowledge of your organizational obligation to your employer and coworkers will not only improve the relationship you have with them, it will also improve your work related personal performance records. And how so you may ask? And the answer to that is, a personal record that shows good attendance and punctuality works in your favor when being considered for promotions and wage increases. I have often seen employees receive disappointing news about their wage increase or attempt at promotion, because of their performance, attendance and punctuality.

So before you call in sick, say you can't work the extra hours or arrive late for work more often than not; think about the effect your actions would have and how it would affect the relationship you have with your peers, employer and the institution. It will not be your ability to do your job that defines your character and value to the institution: your true value will come from you being known to go beyond your immediate tasks, to aid your coworkers and the institution successfully complete theirs. This is what it means to deliver on your obligation to the organization.

So What's My Job Anyway?

By now you should realize that the term "your job" is two parts and has many factors. And the most important aspect of your job being the completion of the job in its entirety. And this comes from you truly understanding what your job is and doing beyond just your tasks to ensure that the company does its job. The other is your tasks itself and doing it in the manner in which you are expected. This is the essence of truly doing your job. So now that you know how to do it, you should also know what it is you have to do. But that's something that I can't tell you and only you would know. And it can get even more confusing because most people will not truly understand the question, what's your job?

When asked, most people say "yeah I know my job". They can also give a short description of their job as in the case of, I'm a taxi driver or a traffic agent. But is that your job? Transporting people or giving out tickets. It clearly is part of your job but it's a fraction of the bigger picture. When you transport a passenger, you are assisting in the bigger transportation system of your community. When you give out tickets you are instrumental in enforcing the traffic laws and maintaining order in the transportation network. Two distinct jobs serving a purpose individually and collectively within the transportation system. That's your job. When you look at your job, always look at the big picture scenario so you can get a better understanding of your role in the process and what you are trying to achieve.

Not all times will the job description and the job tasks be the same. Sometimes there can be differences with the tasks and the expectations as well. But one thing remains clear. Whatever the differences or uncertainty, it is your responsibility to know what exactly is your job, because you will be held accountable for the results.

And why would you be held accountable? Because if you don't know you should ask, and if you don't ask you should know. And it's that simple. The belief of your employer is that you have been given the tools and training to be efficient at your job. This is why it's absolutely important for you to always seek clarity when it comes to your job. And in addition, you should never blame anyone else for you not being able to find out exactly what your job is. You have to be the one instrumental in retrieving the information, and not expecting someone to simply give it to you. Just because you have a problem with part of your task and even if your supervisor is coaching you, he or she cannot read your mind. And even if their assistance is not enough or simply does not work, it is your responsibility to seek further assistance or clarify what is going wrong. As stated before, they are not psychic and they will need as much feedback and interaction from you as possible to come up with the best solution. If there is a part of your job that is proving to be difficult and you do not seek clarity, you will be held responsible for the issue. Furthermore, telling your boss that you did not know will probably be more damaging than you making a mistake. There is no such thing as release of responsibility, due to errors caused by your ignorance to the process. Part of the company's expectation of you is for you to know how to perform your duty, in the manner in-which you are being compensated to do so.

So what happens when you need advice at the spur of the moment and everything seems to conflict with each other? That time when the right decision is not clear and there is no time to make that call to a supervisor. Going with your gut may seem like the best answer in such a situation, but it can prove to be the worst decision you can make.

The truth is that no one has all of the answers. And there will be times when you are in a situation that you have never experienced before. But when faced with this type of situation, the best approach is to try and follow procedure. Providing that you can reach someone, or some other resource to apply procedure to the situation you're dealing with. And if procedure is not applicable, then you apply the core values as long as it does not significantly conflict with procedure. And in most instances it should not. And if procedure and core values do not apply, they use your best judgment that minimizes conflict with procedure and core values.

Your job is a combination of your tasks, expectations and an output or result that's satisfactory. And whenever any aspect of your job is not clear, it is your responsibility to resolve it. Trying to pass blame will not make thing better because you will still have to fix the issue whatever it may be. It's better to use your time and energy to know what has to be done, so you do not have any issues in the future.

I'm In So What's Next?

So everything is working out as planned, or you decided that it's not as bad as you originally thought so you're going to stick it out. Well congrats; you're on your way to charting what will be your life long achievement. Your work career. So now that you're in you have to know what you got yourself into. Well first and foremost, the job can be similar to a school setting if you want to know what it's like and you have no job experience. But the difference is what you will be exposed to. And what exactly will you be exposed to? Well just about any and everything you can think of. Many individuals who are new to the work environment, often say that they were exposed to stuff that they never thought or imagined to exist in the work place. And some of their experiences were weird ones. Some had stories that were so hilarious that I could not stop laughing. Others so heartbreaking, that I could only feel sympathetic for what they had to go through. I can also say that I have had some memorable and unexpected experiences when I first started working. But all in all, I took them for what it's worth; experiences. And I used what was useful and discarded or let go of the negative ones. And it's something you must do as well if you want to survive in the workplace.

By now everyone should know about the work environment and the exposure you are subjected to because we have all heard the stories right? But that's usually as far as it goes, you hear the stories. Almost always you will hear about the exposure and what it did to the person. The cause and effect. What you will hardly ever hear is what the individual's role was especially if the experience was a bad one. And I'm telling you this because one of your biggest exposures will be the experiences of others. And in these situations what you must do is listen, evaluate and learn from the experiences of others. What you must not do is use someone else's bad experience as your own. Never get caught up in another employee's bitterness, and use their poor experience as a starting point for interaction with any other person, task, rule or procedure. It's just not practical and makes you biased before you even dealt with the person or situation.

But why are we talking about this? People tell me about their experiences so what's the big deal? The big deal here is that their exposure can be like toxic radiation, if you do not know how career shattering their experience can be to you. I once had an employee sit with me to discuss an issue related to his performance. Half an hour into the conversation and I still did not get a chance to go over the issue with the employee. And why? Because he felt it necessary to discuss all of the injustices that he had heard of others, and not want to speak about his issue. After we were well into an hour of the session, the final determination was termination.

Now the employee was in shock because everyone else he spoke to was suspended for the infringement and he got terminated. And why did I make the decision to terminate? Well it was simple. The employee did not sit with me to discuss his issue. He sat with me to force or appeal a decision based on the experiences of others. He showed me that he was not willing to take responsibility for his actions, but rather make an attempt to justify his case through the grievances of others. As you can see, it landed him nowhere and this is why we never use the experiences of others as our own.

In other examples, I have dealt with situations where employees would tell me I don't want to work with a certain individual. I would ask, "have you ever worked with the person before"? Their response would be no. I would then say "tell you what; give it a shot, a fair shot without the bias of the other coworkers and then tell me if you don't want to work with that person again". I then say, "at least you won't be going off of a story but an actual experience". And if you can help the person why not? We all could use a little help. And then I would wrap up with put yourself in the other persons shoes. How would you feel if someone was judging you before they even met you? Do you see the damaging effect that being caught up in someone's bad experience can have. And in most of these cases it's the new employee, who is the one subjected to the biased belief. And this could also be part of the exposure that you experience. But never fear. You can overcome just about anything with the right application and mindset. As we continue reading we will learn more about issues and how to deal with them but for now, we will keep our focus on getting in and what to expect.

Now in addition to exposure and experiences you will encounter, you will also be required to perform a task which is essentially your job. Also, your tasks may be similar to school assignments but the difference here is that there are stricter requirements for completing your tasks as expected and when expected. And properly completing your task in the manner and timeframe allowed will make the difference in the kind of employment or length of employment you have. And it's so because in the work environment, it's a give and take. What you have to remember is that with the exception of a volunteer position where you basically give more than you receive, you will be compensated for the work that you do. Yes, your salary is not for coming to work it is for doing work. You don't get paid to do a job; you do your job to get paid. Knowing this, you should always strive to do your best so that you truly deserve your compensation for your work done.

As part of the exposure at work you will also come across employees that tackle their job differently. And you will know who they are because there are folks who work for the company, and some that simply work in the company. The folks who work in the company are the ones who take the approach of I get paid to do my job. Compensation before effort. The ones who work for the company do their job and more before they expect to be compensated. As an entry level employee and one that held a managerial position, I can say with certainty that the employee that takes the approach of doing their job and more, before being compensated will definitely be the one most likely to succeed and excel. So take your job seriously, learn quickly and do what the company expects of you.

The Workplace Arena

The Workplace arena - Are you ready to rumble?

And why rumble, you may ask? And for that I reply why not? The workplace can be as competitive as any other competition and trust me, there are often winners and losers in this arena. And just who are your competitors? Well your peers of course. And it's not only that person who reminds you of your high-school or college nemesis. You know, that person who you want to smirk at every time you edged them in doing something. IT'S EVERYONE. Yep everyone. Even that guy or gal who you feel really good working with and really enjoy their company. Yeah I know, but how can that person, you best bud, be your competitor. After all, you get along just perfectly right!

Each of your peers is your comrade and your opponent in your race to succeed and accomplish your goals. But unlike the wielding of an axe in the arena to behead your opponent and achieve victory, the competitive work environment win or lose, can provide valuable lessons and experiences to you. And you should be mindful that an individual's desire to succeed may not always be harmless because at times it can be destructive to their career as well as their competitors. And also be mindful that competition can be direct or indirect.

So what is the difference between direct and indirect competition. Well direct competition is in your face competition. You want something that someone else wants. And sometimes these competitive environments can become so combative that employees go out of their way to win. And through my experience I have basically observed two ways to gain recognition; out do your opponent or discredit them. Now make no mistake, you may inadvertently discredit someone by out doing them but this is not the manner in which I would like to address. It is the willful intent to discredit someone in an effort to gain recognition that I am addressing, and often enough it is a method used by your peers and something you may encounter in the workplace. Now to succeed by discrediting someone can prove a successful approach to moving up in the workplace, providing you possess the knowledge to do so. However, this approach will more often than not, bring to the individual an expeditious career fall, a career plagued with problems or both. And let me explain how. When you work to achieve your goals in a competitive environment, you gain valuable knowledge and experience in your field. As you develop, you do things more effectively and efficiently and possibly in a manner that makes you stand out amongst your peers. Eventually, your methods may one day grant you a promotion or elevated status within the organization because you simply outdid the competition. This approach to career growth is not so much a safe one but more so an ethical one. Your peers will more than likely honor and respect your work and support you in your new position. Now imagine that you take the approach of trying to discredit someone in order to succeed. You may accomplish your goal of moving up but that's just the easy part. Remember you may need the respect and support of the very same people you discredited to get where you are. Even worse, you may need them to stay where you are. And besides, you now have to prove yourself and bring to the table something better than what you disproved. Trust me when I say it is not easy to fix this situation, especially if you were not allocating time to prove that your methods are better in the first place. So to you the newbie, refrain from adopting the approach of discrediting your peers in order to excel in your career.

Through experience, you will be able to develop the knowledge and skills necessary to ace your competition. But learning and developing your skill and abilities will not be the only criteria to grow because you will work with people you can do what you do, and then some. Ultimately your success will depend on what qualities you bring to the table and your ability to endorse them. And what do I mean by that? Well let me give you an example. Take a look at the stars in the sky, assuming you don't live in the city where the only stars you see are on Billboards. When you look you will see many stars and they all shine. And although they are basically made up of the same elements there are some that shine brighter than others. Probably because they are closer, or maybe because they possess some element that the others don't. Can't say for sure, I am not a scientist. But the one thing I do know is that there are some that catch our attention. And like those stars, that's what you want to do, use what you have to catch the attention of those around you. Gain recognition from your characteristics and the contribution you make to the establishment.

Now as mentioned before, your competitors will come at you from two directions. Directly and indirectly. Indirect competition is when your qualities speak for itself. Great personality, dedication, critical thinking skill etc. Things that people do that bring them recognition that they are not placing emphasis on. I'm almost certain that you have come across someone that's just armed to be the one for the job. Like a class president or sport team captain. They did not even have to campaign to be considered for the position. Their way of speaking, deportment and demeanor had a leadership quality the day you met them. This is what I mean by indirect competition. Things that people do that give them recognition without effort. And in the work environment you will find a lot of this. Now does that mean that you are out of the race? Of course not, but it is something to take into consideration and learn from. It in no way means that you should become like these individuals and it does not mean that it's positive recognition to begin with. It is just an explanation of what indirect competition is and something you may have to deal with. Or something you may possess that gives you an edge over your competitors. Inevitably, it's who we are and what we have to offer to the people and the institution that makes the difference.

The Importance Of Change

So why is it so important to change and continuously do so? Because in the work environment, the absence of change will cause stagnation. And by stagnation, I mean lack of growth and potential. Continued growth and success in the work environment is a result of continued ambition and adaptation. Give some taught to the world of CEO's. One of their most known failures is not adapting to changes in the work environment, business environment, public culture and structure. Staying abreast and adapting to the changes within the work force, clients or customers is a requirement to remain successful in business.

So why is it important to change? Because change will help to ensure that you adjust to the work environment and develop the proper work essentials to do your job.

The workplace can be mentally, physically and emotionally challenging to the inexperienced employee. And not being able to adjust to new situations and environments will ultimately lead to failure. And what does the work environment have to do with my ability to perform? Well just about everything. If your job involves standing for long hours or walking around then there is a physical requirement of your job that you must meet. Or take for instance a job that involves dealing with injury and illness on a daily basis. If you do not have the mental and psychological aptitude to deal with these situations you have to develop it, or you will have a hard time working.

Now there is a saying that "when in Rome, do as the Romans do". And it means if you are in Rome, you have to develop a Roman sense of culture and behavior to get by. This principle is the same as an immigrant living in another country. Eventually, they assimilate into the culture and ethical norms of the country in which they migrated too. And just as there is social culture there is also work place culture.

If you take a look at certain individuals in a certain work environment, you will notice that they almost all have the same personality. For instance, people in law enforcement careers usually have a stern way about them and are often very forward in the way they communicate and their demeanor. And why so? Because their job requires them to be this way. Another example is individuals who work in the judicial setting such as lawyers and judges. Their level of confidence can often be viewed as arrogance and their body language and speech is often charismatic and alluring. I am almost certain that all of these individuals probably did not have these characteristics when they first started working. But their present image is a result of their assimilation into the somewhat required characteristic of an individual working in the judicial system. Individuals who has fully adjusted to their work environment.

So just how much of yourself do you change? How much change is considered enough? Well the answer is never that clear and it is also important to know that too much emphasis on change can have a negative effect on your personality as well.

As we mentioned earlier, immigrants conform to the social and ethical norms of their new country, but some of them also retain their culture and ethics from their country of origin. And how can they do so? They do so because they have developed a positive balance of their old way of life and their new way of life. And for you it would mean adjusting to the new work culture but being able to maintain your identity. You will do what you must to adjust to the new environment, but you will not become so enveloped, that the new identity becomes your permanent one.

You probably have heard the term "taking the job home". And it means that an individual is so into his or her job that they maintain this work character when they are not at work. Because of their new demeanor and characteristics, they are often descried as acting differently or strange. Their friends and family members start to avoid them and try to interact with them as infrequently as possible. This is why it's important to never take the job home. You should always keep work at work and home at home unless it is beneficial to integrate the two aspects of your personality. As a professional, you should know and be able to control two personalities and know when to turn each one off and on. Failure to do so could come at a grave cost, and potentially ruin your relationships with family and friends. And I do not believe that there is any job that is worth more that family and friends.

So now that you know why you should change let's discuss what you should change about yourself. You change what's necessary to adapt to the work environment to perform in the appropriate manner. And what is the appropriate manner; it is the expected conduct, contribution and demeanor desired by your establishment. In other words, you change as much as necessary to become the right fit.

A perfect example of being the right fit is recently I visited a gym with a relative of mine. As I was filling out my visitors form, I noticed that a gentleman was applying for a job as a personal trainer. I happened to overhear him speaking about his qualifications and I must admit it was impressive. But for the physique of the individual, there were some doubts in the connection to his career of choice. Basically he let himself go. Now it does not mean he will not get the job, but compared to the other trainers at the gym, who can be compared to professional bodybuilders and pro athletes, he had his work cut out for him. After all, wouldn't you prefer to train with someone that you would like to look like as compared to someone that looks like you? A feature as simple as appearance can make the difference between success and failure. And even though the new trainer may have more experience, the trainers with less experience but better physical appeal would develop a greater client base.

So now that you understand the need for change, you now need to know what you should change. And no, not everything about yourself, just the necessary components to fit in your new environment. And these components can be anything from mental, physical and emotional characteristics to behavior, communication and demeanor. For example, if you want to be a physical trainer and you were out of shape what would you have to do? Get fit right? Or if you wanted to be a soldier or police officer and had a fear of firearms. What would you have to do? Get over it right, because the potential for firearms use is a requisite of this careers. Or what if you want to be a doctor and cannot handle death very well. How will you comfort and inform family members of the bad news if you show emotional compromise? Unless you were born to do the job as they say, then it may be necessary for you to change some aspect of you personality, physicality, mindset or demeanor. Or any combination of these and more to be able to do the job.

Although you may know what to change, the method may not always be right in front of you. For example, if you want to be a runner and you are overweight, certain life changes will be obvious such as diet and exercise. But even with the knowledge of what needs to be done, how can you be sure you're doing it right? I'm sure we can agree that not all diets are the same and not all exercise or training is the same. As they say, results may vary. So what the sensible want to be runner would do is evaluate the sources of information to find the right diet and exercise regimen, to suit his or her desire or need.

Two of the greatest sources of information to evaluate your need for change are advice and criticism. Now should you change based on all advice and criticism? Of course not, because just like diet and exercise, not all advice will be good advice and not all criticism will be constructive criticism. So what you need to do is take heed to all, but evaluate them to find the information that may be beneficial to you, your team and the institution. Now from these two sources, I have always found criticism to be the most beneficial. Especially that of my competitors who would critique my character, performance and work ethics to its fullest. And why should you care about what they think or say about you? Because their viewpoint may be the most in-debt evaluation of all of your weaknesses. In the next chapter entitled the reality of perception, we will address this topic in more detail but for now, give great consideration to how you competitors view you and evaluate the information to find advice that may benefit you.

Change is inevitable. And any employee, who does not embrace and prepare themselves for change, is preparing for their own demise. But as harsh as it might seem, change is not something you should fear. It is what has shaped your present and ultimately your future. So when you embrace change. And hone your ability to properly evaluate your strengths and weaknesses. Coupled with constantly working towards improving each of them will help to ensure your upward mobility, longevity and future success.

The Reality Of Perception

So what do we mean by the reality of perception? Well to find the answer we must first find out the meaning of perception and according to Webster, it is "a result of perceiving". And just in case you were wondering who Webster is, it's a dictionary. So now we ask, what is perceiving? And once again we seek out Webster and his infinite wisdom to which his answer to the question is "to attain awareness or understanding of". So what is perception: it is a taught or conclusion based on what an individual is aware of or presumes to understand.

So how does this apply to the workplace and of what importance is it to you? And in short it has everything to do with the workplace and you. You see, no matter who you think you are, what matters is who everyone else thinks you are. Now don't *perceive* this message to be an attack on your individuality. It is simply intended to make you aware of the importance of how the way people view you, can impact your character in the work environment. I once asked someone, if ten people see you as a jerk does that make you're a jerk? And the person responded, "no I'm not a jerk, do you think so? And I said to him, of course your. But then I asked, does the opinion of those ten people count? And the person replied, if I care about them or know them I guess so. And now I ask you what do you think? Do you believe that the opinions of other people count and should we ever be concerned with how we are viewed by others?

The work environment is very different from any other environment that you are accustomed to. And unlike a social home setting or interaction with your friends or the general public where you can be yourself, the work environment can present certain challenges if you are viewed in a negative way by your coworkers. In the work environment, it is important for you to assess how you are viewed by others and their general perception of you. And why is it so important for you to be concerned with how people view you? Especially when everyone who already knows you think you are a swell individual. Well, to understand this you would have to understand the correlation of an individual's character in relation to his or her environment or social setting.

Let's take a look at the family environment. This is where you would most likely find the most love, appreciation and kindness. Your family and other relatives will give you a high level of support for your endeavors, and would be highly sympathetic and forgiving of your mistakes and indiscretions. You would most likely have a similar relationship with your friends who may be even more sympathetic of your wrongdoings and indiscretions. The work environment however, is very different from that of family and friends and tolerance for wrongdoing and indiscretion is highly unacceptable. So what may be deemed as acceptable conduct, language and deportment by people who view you as an individual of sound judgment and character may not be the same in the work environment. In the work environment, if you are viewed as an individual of unsound character, then this is what will shape the relationship you have with your peers and bosses.

So let's visit a scenario. A man riding on a horse is accompanied by a pregnant woman and an old lady. The pregnant lady and the old woman seem to be struggling to keep up and as they get to the village, the local folks were not too happy with what they saw. As they ride into town, the villagers start making remarks to the man such as "your no gentleman, how could you let the women walk". One man even went as far as to try and stop the man from riding the horse because he just couldn't stand the sight of the two women walking. With so much attention and people actually trying to stop them the pregnant woman finally said "don't blame my husband, he cannot hear very well and he only has one leg".

Paints a whole different picture now doesn't it? This is the power of perception and this is what perception is. A belief based on what someone understands about something. Had they known that the man only had one leg they would have understood why he and not the women had to ride the horse. And this is the reality of perception when it comes to you. If you create that vision for them to believe then this is now your truth. This is now who they know you to be. This is how they see you. And just like the man riding the horse you may not have a chance to correct the assumption of who you are. Once that train of a negative viewpoint of you starts going, it's very hard to turn it around.

So what can you do to help ensure that people do not have a negative perception of you? Well ask yourself this question, if you were part of that traveling crew, what could you have done differently to guide a conclusion other than the one the villagers arrived at?

With the exception of a sign draped around the man that says I have one leg, I can't think of anything else they could have done. But who knows, maybe you can. The point here is that perception can be a powerful source to give identity to someone and it is for this reason, why you should always be mindful of how you being viewed can work against you. I have dealt with many investigations of employees where perception was the key factor that led to a complaint or accusation. And it's not that the employees were doing anything wrong, they were just not aware of how they were being viewed or analyzed at the time. Or they did not pay any mind to the fact that, they being viewed in a certain way could be an issue. And unlike the man on the horse, it may not always be as easy as to give an explanation and everyone understands. Or you cannot say that you just don't care what people think about you. You have to be concerned and you have to care. It's your work character that they are evaluating to be good or bad and often enough their opinion will matter. Especially if it's more than one person saying the same thing or having the same opinion about you, your conduct or your performance.

So always remember to safeguard your character. And be mindful of how someone can perceive you and the effects of their opinions. Before you do anything, think ten steps ahead to see how the end result can be perceived by others. And it's also good advice to consider the opinions of others and how it may affect you before you act.

The People At Work

The work place can be a melting pot of different peoples, personalities and behaviors. All of whom may not take to you and you to them. Furthermore, all of you are in competition with each other whether you tend to believe so or not, and it's something you must take heed too. But how do you identify friend from foe? How do you know who is on your side and who you need to be wary of?

In keeping it simple, there will be people you work well with and people you don't. However, this may not be the initial setting because as time passes by, you may start to develop relationships with people you never imagined you would and end relations with folks you were cool with in the beginning.

There are several verses in a song titled "who the cap fit's" by the late singer songwriter Bob Marley, that's very applicable to the work environment. In particular, there is a verse in the song that states "your worst enemy could be your best friend and your best friend your worst enemy". It is with this knowledge that we should expect everyone to be an equal adversary and ally. And what exactly does this mean? Well, it does not mean to make your enemies your friends and make your friends your enemies. It simply means that people you consider your friends could actually be your enemies and people you consider your enemies could one day become your friends. So why is this of importance to me you may ask? Because your ability to grow and maintain a positive work environment depends on it.

To answer this question, it may be a better process to tackle this situation if we broke it in two: dealing with your enemies and dealing with friends. But before we do so, I think the first thing we should do is change the descriptions of the parties involved. Instead of saying enemy as the song implies, we will use the word rival. And instead of friend, we will use the word associate or acquaintance. It's important to correctly describe the parties because more likely than not, who we describe as your enemy is not your enemy and you describe as friend is not your friend. Because in the workplace, all you really have is coworkers. You don't need enemies. And friends or friendship is something that will come later.

So let's tackle the rival. If you see this person in their true light as a rival and not an enemy, then you can adhere to a professional and adult like approach to resolving conflicts. Often enough, young individuals such as yourself often exaggerate or misrepresent a situation and attach an emotional reaction and description to a conflict. For the most part, and unless this person or group is out to physically hurt you, then they are nothing more than a rival. And just what makes them a rival? There are many reasons. And the fact that all of you are striving to achieve and grow in the same work environment, is reason enough for someone to be considered a rival. And in turn, most conflicts are born of different opinions and approaches rather that hateful thoughts and deeds. I have witnessed many times as a supervisor that employees complain about other employees because of a different viewpoint. And when left unsolved, these subtle differences can fester creating an atmosphere of animosity between coworkers.

When involved in these continued conflicts, it is usually at this point that we categorize these individuals as our enemies. But all you really have is two people not wanting to work with each other or in each other's presence because they do not agree on something. Hardly an enemy. And the effort you make to sustain the hostility is more than the one required to resolve it. So it's better to seek to resolve conflicts because in the end, it's really not worth it.

And as I mentioned before, working towards maintaining positive relationships with your peers is an essential part of building your value within the institution. You don't have to like someone to be able to work with them or try to make a friend out of the situation. Because you may not want to have that kind of relationship with the other person and vice versa. What you don't need is someone making an effort to have a problem with you. Because it only means that you will have to make an effort to counteract the issue, or explain to everyone why there is none. Which is ultimately a waste of valuable mental energy that you could be using towards other productive causes. And I can assure you that dealing with work related conflicts can be very stressful, even to the point where you can jeopardize your employment. So the less of this sort of nonsense you have to deal with the better it is for you.

Now make no mistake, just because someone has a good work relationship with you, does that mean that they are not your rival. So with this fact, it brings us to the part of the song that says "your best friend can be your worst enemy". And as before, it is important to categorize your co-worked appropriately. Considering your coworker to be your friend can be very misleading and in some instances detrimental to your character and continued employment. Sounds sort of farfetched don't it? But ask yourself, what is a friend? Well according to dictionary.com, a friend is "a person attached to another by feelings or affection or personal regard, a person who gives assistance or supports, a person who is on good terms with another". Now I think you would agree that if you are that persons' friend and that person is you friend, then it is safe to say that you have a friendship right?

But let's examine that. Say for instance you are cool with a coworker because you consider her to be your friend and you start telling her about yourself. You engage in conversations about your personal life and your family problems. Your friend listens and gives you the best advice you ever heard. Their advice was very sound and everything worked out well for you. So you start pumping out more and more information until one day you hear what you told your friend from someone else. Low and behold, now everyone knows everything about you and now you are mad at your friend. Now ask yourself. Would any of your real friends do something like that to you and if so, do you think it would have an impact on your work environment? And when I say your real friends, I mean the ones you had before you started working at the company. The ones you went to school with or grew up with in your neighborhood. These people are your real friends. The people you work with are your coworkers and only with time and experiences, should you consider them your friends.

Similar to the social network Facebook, do you really think that the folks with five hundred or six hundred friends and more are actually friends with these people? And if you happen to have over five hundred friends on Facebook, are they really your friends?

Would you share your most private information with half of those so called friends of yours? Of course not. So why would it make sense for anyone to develop so much trust in so little time, to consider a coworker a friend. So the correct term would be associate. And with knowledge of them being associates, it should make it easier for you to safeguard yourself.

So how exactly do you distinguish friend from foe? Well my friend there is no magic formula or equation to simplify this process. But as a general rule ask yourself, if it's your enemy, is it worth having a civil non rival relationship with this person and if I do, what are the consequences. And if someone is your friend, is this someone I can trust and will this friendship come back to haunt me someday. With decisions that can go back and forth on trying to decide who is on your side or not, the best thing to do is play it safe. And to play it safe you try to avoid having friends and enemies and just get along with everyone. Try to remain neutral and build solid relationships with everyone, even the ones who are your rivals. Because you never can tell when the person or people you don't get along with may be the ones who you have to lean on.

Peers - From Associate To Friend

So I have been working with this person for a couple of months now and they seem to be really cool. We share a lot of our personal stuff and we have even hung out a couple of times. I have even met some of her family and friends and they all seem cool as well. My friend has also met some of my friends and family members and they all get along just fine. Can I consider this person my friend?

The last time I checked people at work are regular people and as regular people they can be your friend. But with all things being fair, people at work are regular people and not all can qualify as friend. And why not? Because to find the answer you should ask yourself, what makes a person qualify as being your friend. Whatever measurement, standard or in the extreme, your personal formula you use for calculating the qualities of friendship, it's the same with any group of people you encounter. Be its strangers, your basketball club, church, bar, restaurant or at work, you make friends based on agreeable behaviors between yourself and the other person. The only difference being the environment whereby the friendship was kindled.

The bar, restaurant and basketball club are all considered sociable meeting places and the friendships you create are of a sociable nature. On the other hand, the workplace is considered a professional environment. And although the friendships you make there can be the same as the ones you make in other group setting, the difference is of significance when it comes to the negative aspects of a friendship.

Friendships are great when they are great. And even if we add all of the great quotes as they relate to friendship and the resolution of problems, problematic friendships in the workplace is a whole different ballgame. And its resolution is not as easy as some of the advice given in these quotes. Just walk away, true friendships last forever, a good friend is like, you know them when times are hard etc. etc. etc. Not that easy and never that simple when you work with the person. So before you decide to embark on a friendship crusade. You should always take great consideration for not only the positive aspects of the friendship, but the potentially negative aspects of the friendship as well. Because things can go from being great to being nightmarish in the blink of an eye, with major consequence for you.

Your job should be of importance to you because it helps with your economic structure. Knowing this, it is also important to know what issues can affect your job and what you must do to minimize these issues. Friendships or problematic ones can be one of these issues and you must be totally aware of the consequence it can cause in the work environment. However, what we will not do is look at how negative friendships affect you personally. We all have experienced a negative friendship and it's the same regardless of the setting, be it social or work related. What we will discuss is how a negative friendship will affect you in the work setting and how it's not so easy to resolve it, as compared to a social setting.

The friendship is not working out so let's just decide not to be cool anymore. Works great for a friendship borne of a social disposition. I'll stop going to the basketball club, the gym or the park that you go to and just join another one. That's great and problem solved because I can remove myself from the environment, thus ending the friendship. But how do you do that in the work related scenario of a friendship gone wrong? Leaving the job and going to another is one way. But is it a practical solution? Is it a wise thing to do? Are there drawbacks to making such a decision such as economical or career negatives? Even if the other company was to hire you immediately and you do not suffer any break in employment or salary, is it a logical solution to resolving the issue? I would definitely say no and leaving your present job because of a problematic friendship should be a situation that you never get yourself into. Simply put, it's not that easy to remove yourself from the environment when a friendship goes wrong.

Can you imagine the tension and uneasy feeling of working with someone that your friendship ended horribly? How long before that tension starts to show in your task and performance. Before you know it, you or your friend could be requesting a change of partner, department or location, just to avoid further interaction with the individual. And the change would usually come at the cost of the person making the request for the change. So if you made the request for a change, be prepared to be the one to change your partner, shift, department, location etc. Imagine if others started picking up on the issue, or your now former friend starts broadcasting the events that led up to the end of your friendship. It could be something of a personal nature that happened to you or someone you know, and now your former friend is airing out your business. And we all know how rumors work. Misconstrued information of the facts leading to different factors, events and conclusions. Could get ugly right? Certainly one of those situations that you would rather not have to deal with, but certainly a condition of a work related friendship that you must be prepared to deal with. And I say deal with because this is a condition that can arise as a result of having friends at work.

And what if it did get ugly? Could end up being damaging to your career right? I have witnessed situations where people have lost their jobs or opportunities to advance their career because of failed work related friendships or the issues associated with them. All of them, never thinking that the person that they were friends with could do some of the things that they did. Even in situations where we believe that the issue is minor, we never can tell where it can lead or if it can escalate into something bigger. You have to remember that people are people no matter what group they are associated with. And as friends, they can bring both positive and negative to the friendship.

So far it appears that work related friendships are something that everyone should stay away from and just consider each other as peers or acquaintances. But that is not the message here. It's not a message of not making friends. The message here is not about how to fix broken friendships or avoid having one in the first place. It's about the complications of work related friendships and you being aware of them.

Making friends is a good thing when it's working out and brings the same rewards of any other friendship. I have come to have friends in the workplace of who were peers, bosses and subordinates and those friendships were just as rewarding as the ones I had from any other social background. They had their bad moments like any other friendship, but they were always controlled and applicable to the workplace. And it was applicable because it was based on nothing other than our friendship. Which was simple and uncomplicated. And how was it controlled? It was controlled because of the pace at which the friendship grew and the input that I allowed as part of the friendship.

The consideration for friendship should be gradual and in stages. As your friendship grows and you build trust and comfort with the other person, you can decide how open you want to be. And that's the key. You can socialize, hang out and get involved in activities with your work friends just as you would with any other friend of yours, but you don't have to share every intimate detail about yourself. They don't have to know your personal problems or what's going on with your family or friends. In fact, the less they know the better in the initial bonding and as time goes on, you add whatever makes you feel comfortable. In small chunks preferably.

Being open and revealing everything about you is not a requisite for being cool or being a friend. And anyone who has a problem with that is probably fishing for more than just your friendship. Your new work friends don't have to know what your other friends know. And vice versa. They don't have to meet your family and friends, your spouse, intended and children. They don't have to see you as relaxed and comfortable as you are with your friends and family because there may be some things about yourself that you do not want to expose them too. At least not yet, so it's best you keep your guard up and maintain a high standard even when socializing. Now you could if you want to, but these open friendships should take time and not be part of the initial friendship. Keeping it uncomplicated, with only the relevant things about you is the best way to approach a work friendship. It prevents unwanted information about you from being disseminated. And if it does not work out, there isn't much collateral damage left in its wake.

Supervisor - Boss Or Buddy

So there is this particular supervisor at work who seems to be very friendly and very approachable. She greets everyone she meets as if she is ecstatic to see them. She jokes with everyone including you and for the most part, you seem to have a pleasant work relationship.

One day you see her at a casual hangout that some of the employees put together and she is really down to earth. She is having just as much fun and could be deemed the life of the party so to speak. There was even a time that you invited her to one of your social functions and she came. Certainly one can only assume that you are friends and that your work relationship is meaningful. Well if you are thinking this way then you are correct. Or at least you are correct to assume you are because she is making the extra effort to have some sort of interaction beyond the workplace.

You can certainly be friends with your supervisor, manager or boss and there is nothing wrong with that. In fact, I would advise any employee to try and have a relationship with his or her boss beyond the formality of work tasks and communication based solely on work. What better position is there to be in than one where your boss personally knows you? That's freaking awesome, and can certainly make your life a bit easier when it comes to the work place.

Now please be mindful that when I say friends or meaningful relationships beyond work, I am not saying that you should make jokes and invite them to parties in an effort to generate a meaningful relationship. Joking and hanging out can be part of it if your boss is ok with joking and socializing with you, but don't push this issue or make it obvious that you are craving a casual friendship type relationship. An open communication channel where you can speak to your boss freely, and not only during his or her work hours can also suffice.

Now getting the friendship going is one thing, keeping the friendship going is another. There are certain situations that can dissolve your friendship and one such situation, is if you give your boss a feeling that you are in it for your own benefit. So in order to not give off that feeling, there are some don'ts when it comes to developing a good boss-employee friendship.

First and foremost, you must understand that your friendship with your boss is not an open request line. Your boss is not your personal genie in a bottle that every time you rub, they come out and grant you three wishes. If you give your boss the impression that for every conversation there is a possibility that you will have a request, you can kiss that friendship goodbye. Second, is the fact that the friendship you have with your boss is not your personal get out of jail free card. And if you do not know what that means, it means that your boss will not be there to bail you out if you get in trouble. In fact, the boss may even be harder on you because of his or her level of disappointment in you and their expectations of you. Third on the list of things that you should know is, your boss is not a problem box. Now I know before in past chapters I said that it's ok to bring your problems to your boss and she would be the best source to do it with. But it doesn't mean that because your boss is now your buddy, that she wants to hear about your problems every chance you get. Even when the boss says it's ok "I'm always working" you should not do it. When a boss says I'm always working, it's not something you should take literally or believe it's a green light for you. She is just trying to be professional and polite. But I guarantee that if you think I'm wrong, try it and see just how fast your boss can be unreachable and permanently occupied. And it's not that they're fake or that they just don't care, it's just that they're human and will need a break from work and dealing with issues, especially someone else's.

The next thing you should know is your friendship with your boss is not a magic wand. If you have an issue, she may not be able to easily make it go away or fix it. In fact, if you have a problem you might very well continue to have the problem. Your boss does not have to move at any other pace than he or she would, if they were dealing with an employee that they have never interacted with. Friendship does not grant you entitlement for anything.

Finally, don't put your boss in an awkward position. Not at work and especially outside of work. When at work, don't be a drama magnet or the living example of Murphy's Law where anything that can go wrong will go wrong when it comes to you. Don't be friends with your boss and find yourself in her office every week to discuss an issue and receive disciplinary action. When out of work socializing, don't post pictures of your boss socializing without her consent. Don't act a fool in the presence of your boss then post to your time line with pics; saying in your tag that your boss was there. Even if you think there is nothing wrong with it your boss most likely will, and she will remove herself from your friendship sooner rather than later.

If you steer clear of these issues or any other situation that can put your boss in an uncomfortable situation, you will be able to maintain a wonderful friendship. And never make your boss have to work at maintaining your friendship. Your boss will be your buddy as long as you can prove to be an employee that he or she, does not have to manage in friendship. Which means, if your friendship proves to be work it will come to an abrupt end and I can assure you it will.

The boss will always try his or her best to interact with everyone, but the level of interaction and the amount of interaction can increase if you happened to make it on their buddy list. Now rest assured that the boss being your buddy does come with perks but there is some work involved and it's not as easy as you think it is. When the boss becomes your buddy, she is saying that you are the kind of person that will uphold the integrity of the institution and the credibility of the boss. With that being said, there are some ground rules that apply to you and you must adhere to, if you want to be considered for a good buddy relationship with your boss.

For example, you will have to be an above average employee. Meaning, you will have to be the kind of person that the boss can say without a shadow of a doubt, that you are company material, with an aura about you that says you are destined for greatness. Well maybe not so much but enough to show that you have exemplary standards and characteristics. You will also have to be a team player. Remember when we spoke about the difference between "your job" and "the job" in a past chapter. Being a team player is about getting the job done and not just your tasks, and the boss will definitely like to know that you're not only her friend, but also someone she can count on when times get tough.

And lastly we come to the book of the dammed. Or otherwise known as the black listed book. This is where you should never be and if you are, chances of kindling any friendship with your boss will prove to be slim to none. Because the boss has her reputation and credibility to uphold, she will not want to be known for being in league with a troublemaker. And rightly so. Because an individual's credibility is something that he or she will have to protect if they want to succeed in the workplace. And hopefully you will also understand the need to protect your credibility, and keep out of the black listed book.

So far there have only been your efforts and the don'ts of befriending a supervisor. So what's in it for you is probably what you're asking yourself right now. Well there is a lot in it for you and if you do succeed, you can reap the benefits as well.

So here are some examples of the positives involved with a supervisor being your friend. A supervisor as a friend is a permanent helpline that you can use in times of need. Now this is different from the personal requests where you want something, whereas in this situation, you need something. But you must always try to keep it simple and use only when necessary to avoid an overbearing feeling. In addition, did you ever want an open answer on something? Well as a friend of a supervisor, you may be able to get feedback that is not structured with political and diplomatic consideration based on a workplace setting. She can filter out the niceties or work place discretion to give you real feedback.

One of the best attributes of having a boss as a friend is having a coach or mentor. Employees, who are fortunate enough to become friends with their boss, can gain valuable exposure in the true processes, behaviors and actions of management. This exposure can give you a better understanding of the management role as it relates to business, and a better understanding and approach to the way you view your job. You can also be privy to lots of valuable information that the average employee is not aware of. Essentially placing you in-the-know.

So as you can see, being friends with your supervisor, manager or boss can be rewarding. And although you may have to make an effort, the benefits of having a boss as a friend sure outweigh the effort it takes to create and maintain the friendship. And the more you are known for being a model employee the less you will have to work at it. And remember, the boss is a person just like you, and your work generated friendship can be as regular and rewarding as any other.

Customers And Clients

As part of your job, dealing with customers and clients can make up a significant part of the people factor. Also, as part of your job of dealing with clients or customers you would have been told in some form or the other, that the customer is always right. And it is the golden rule for providing excellent customer service and overall customer satisfaction. And it's that simple. Know it, breathe it, live it and love it. And when in doubt, always remember that the customer is always right.

Now this is not a statement based on facts derived from solid data. It is simply an approach to dealing with anything, be it a discrepancy, an issue or situation that arises during you interaction with a customer or client. The ultimate GOAL being, the satisfactory level of service experienced by the customer.

Positive interaction with clients and customers will be essential to the sustainability of the business and an expectation the company will have of you. And some companies value the interaction between employees and customers to the extent of giving out awards, prizes and bonuses for positive feedback. Some customers can be so much fun to deal with, that it can be tempting to pursue friendship beyond the customer-employee relationship. But it's never a good idea to make a client or customer a friend. You can develop close acquaintance with them but that's as far as it should go. Sometimes a client or customer is so pleased with your service that he or she makes a personal request for you to assist them. They may know your name, have your direct contact and even come to know some things about you through your conversations that other customers don't. And there is nothing wrong with that. As long as you understand the limit of customer or client-employee relationships and just how acquainted you can become. Sharing intimate information about yourself, personal contact info and engaging in social meetings beyond the workplace should be avoided at all cost. Imagine how uncomfortable it would be to hear your boss say that a client mentioned you said that the item was overpriced. And this conversation took place in an out-of-work setting. That could certainly put your job in jeopardy. Wouldn't you agree? And it is for this reason why it's best to keep customers and clients as their names apply.

Customers and clients can be great and can also make your work day go by much easier. But that's one side of the coin when it comes to dealing with them. On the flip side, customers and clients can be hard to deal with and make your day seem like hell. The worst day of your life so to speak and to the point where you feel like quitting. But you should never let customers get to you and don't take their rants as a personal attack against you.

Even if you messed up their order. You know, you brought out fish when they asked for chicken. You gave them the wrong shoe size and in the wrong color. I can only imagine the magnitude of the customer's displeasure and their conduct when they speak to you. Yeah you messed up, but don't let it get to you. Even in situations where it was 100% your fault and you know that the customer is unhappy because of it; don't take it personal. I know it may be hard to do but try your best to let it go. When you take it personal, you can make the situation worse. You lose sight of the ultimate GOAL which is the satisfactory experience of the customer. So breathe. Compose yourself, and try to fix the issue.

Keeping customers and clients happy and building strong meaningful relationships with them will benefit you, the customers and clients alike. And when things go wrong, here is a simple strategy you can use to remedy the situation and possibly prevent future instances. Remember what the ultimate GOAL is. Happy satisfied customer and a pleasurable customer experience.

Think GOAL

So when there is an issue. Think GOAL. Because a goal signifies an end point, a status towards a victory, a positive score. A desired ending. The first two letters in GOAL relates to the customer, situation, and resolution, the second two letters relates to the company, evaluation of the problem and the solution.

G - Give the complainant or issue your full attention. Stop what you're doing if you can or soon thereafter. Listen attentively and apologize for the poor experience.

O - Offer a solution. If you can resolve it do so. If not, escalate the issue to a supervisor or manager so they can attempt to resolve the issue.

A - Assess the discrepancy, complaint or issue to see what went wrong and identify the cause or origin of the problem

L - Learn from it. The definition of insanity is doing the same thing and expecting a different result. Use the results of your assessment to find a workable solution to prevent it from happening again.

Houston We Have A Problem, I Hate My Boss

So you have come to the conclusion that you hate your boss and this is because of? Yes I am asking you a question. What happened for you to get to the point of hating your boss? Did he or she do something to you that brought you to this point of hate? It has to be because I can't see any other reason for you hating your boss.

The truth is it doesn't take much for an employee to hate their boss and it's usually because the boss is just being the boss. And when the boss has to be the boss, especially when he or she is disciplining or need to get a point across; it is not always taken lightly by the employee. The hate can come from other areas as well such as the bosses tone, demeanor or body language. It can also come from situations where the boss fell short on something that the employee was waiting on such as an evaluation or recommendation. All of which can escalate an employee to the point of going postal on his or her boss.

So is there something wrong with hating a boss? Well I would say there is a lot. I highly doubt that you went through all that trouble to get the job, to ultimately hate your boss. Especially if the boss does not feel that way towards you and he or she is oblivious to how you truly feel. Even worse, is when you hate a boss and he or she did not do anything to you or at least not intentionally. In my career, I have heard of situations where an employee hated me and I was baffled by the news. Even worse, it was an employee that I knew that I did a hell of a lot for. So before you go on an agenda of hate there are some things you must take into consideration.

I can recall a time in my earlier years when I had a boss that I absolutely despised. Now for what it's worth, I had some culpability in our failed relationship but I always had the feeling that my boss had it in for me. Looking back on that situation, I can only come to the conclusion that my boss was more disappointed in my behavior rather than feeling hate towards me. And I can collaborate this feeling based on my own situations where an employee of mine had hate for me.

But my feelings towards the situation and the employee were based on me being disappointed, and not any sort of hate as he or she might have come to believe.

Peering back into the pass and evaluating my own problems when it came to my boss, I realized that there were certain factors that were obvious, but not obvious to me. For example, I and my boss were not the same. He was my boss and that meant that he could administer disciplinary measures towards me. He was also in a position to say no to my requests. His position also gave him the authority to give criticism and be upset about my performance. And why not, I have found a way to put myself on his naughty list so it's fairly reasonable why he should come down on me. Even if you have never worked before, you can compare this situation to a teacher that you did not get along with. At that time, I'm sure you felt like your hate for the teacher was justifiable based on your interaction. But what about now? Do you think that if you could go back with the mature mindset that you presently hold, your feelings towards the teacher would be the same? And did you know that when you put effort into hating your boss, it can also affect your work? This happens because you take things personal and every instruction given is an attack on you. You spend time evaluating his or her words and actions to see if there is any underlying treat or loophole, to challenge their position and directive. All of which by the way is pointless, and will ultimately get you nowhere. And if you ever want to grow, having conflicts with your boss is a sure way to throw every chance you got out the door.

Sometimes the hate we feel for our boss can become personal. We feel like the boss did something wrong to us and we hold on to it. This issue becomes the fuel to sustain our hate and in-turn, we become self-sustaining hate generating employees. This my friend is the worst type of hate because it can create a mental prison that causes you, to not be in the mindset to resolve your issue. Your continued hate will concretize your belief that the boss did you wrong, and you may start isolating yourself from your boss. And what if your boss starts noticing the change in your relationship and the fact that you are minimizing your interaction with him or at all cost? If your boss picks up on changes, he may also withdraw and keep your work relationship strictly business. And there is nothing worse that someone disliking you and you know it, but you don't know why.

On every angle, hating your boss does not make anything better for you. In fact, it can only make things worse. And it doesn't matter if you are right or wrong. The only thing that matters is it's more beneficial to have a positive and communicative relationship than to not. Now one can argue that they can hold two opposing mindsets and not like their boss but maintain a professional work relationship. And the more you think you have it under control is the more obvious you can make it. Trust me, it will show. Having a good work relationship goes beyond simply being professional at work and there is no such thing as trying to act like you're ok with someone. It's either you are or you aren't. So it's best to let go of the hate, work at resolving the issue and develop or restore a positive work relationship with your boss.

And besides, your boss really does not owe you anything. So if your anger is based on a request, especially one of a personal nature such as a reference letter or a potential work contact, you need to get over it as soon as possible. Your boss does not have to be accommodating all of the time and can tell you no. And even if the boss says yes, you cannot always assume that he will give your request priority over everything else. So here's a good hint; if it's important to you, follow up to ensure that everything is still going as planned. That way, you can track the progress and or make alternate plans. Further saving you, some unnecessary boss hating energy.

And by the way, did this ever cross your mind; what if your boss made a mistake? As a boss I know that I have. What if your boss did not do something for you because he simply forgot? I know as a boss I did forget to do stuff or fulfill a request from an employee. Even if it's the most important thing in the world to you does that justify your reason for hating your boss? I think you have all right to be upset but to maintain hate is going overboard, especially if it was an error. What you should always remember is the boss is not mistake proof. He makes mistakes and fall short of tasks and responsibilities just like anyone else.

But how will you know if you do not work at resolving the issue? There is nothing wrong with having a conversation with your boss about something that is bothering you. He certainly will not have an issue speaking to you about an issue. And what if the boss knew that he or she was wrong and wanted to make amends but you made yourself unapproachable. It becomes worse when you take it so personal, that you don't even try to meet with your boss on his or her request because you are consumed by your hate. All of which are actions not conducive to creating a pleasurable work relationship.

I hope that throughout your career, you never get to such a place because you will certainly be going to a place for which it is hard to return from. Developing hate to such an extent shows a lack in your ability to maintain your professionalism, and your susceptibility to become emotionally compromised. And as with any work relationship, working towards making them better will always be the best course of action.

My Boss Hates Me

In most cases where there isn't an obvious reason to suspect that your boss hates you, it's usually a feeling of your boss hating you before you reciprocate the feeling. However, and more often than not, it's hard to tell if your boss really hates you. Now I know to some professionals reading this book that hate would be a strong word but for what's its worth, we will use hate to define the situations in its harshest form. And not necessarily to reflect deep seated animosity towards you.

Now you believe that your boss does not like you. But why do you think so? Did your boss tell you "I hate you" or is this an assumption? Do you have irrefutable evidence to support your notion that the boss is out to get you? The truth is that we often generalize relationships into two categories of good and bad, with no variation or midpoint. Now I'm not saying that this is how the average person views relationships, but it's usually the medium for evaluating a boss employee relationship.

As a manager, I have heard people say that I did not like them. Or through third party information that I did not like someone. And that was strange to me because if I didn't like someone, the one person who would know should be me. At least I think so. And here's the kicker, I didn't even know who the person was. I saw the person a couple of times and probably said hi to her. But that was it. I hated this person with all that I have in me and I didn't even know it. Asleep at my own wheel. My hate game is so good that I'm hating and don't even know it.

But seriously, clearly we can see that the individual came to a conclusion on their own that I did not like her. I could only think that the reason she felt that way could have been because I did not greet her with a smile or didn't say much to her, as I probably did with someone else. But nevertheless, I had nothing against her but she believed I did.

Now I have been fortunate enough to be on both ends of the employee spectrum of having a boss and being a boss. And not boss as in owner, but someone in-charge and with enough authority to make major decisions. And just like the employee who taught that I did not like her, I too have had the feeling that my boss did not like me. Yep, I sure did. And everything in my gut told me that my boss did not like me. But did that make it true?

Now similar to what I explained as the possible reason for my employee feeling like I did not like her, was the reason that I felt that my boss did not like me. My boss would interact with others in a different way than he did with me. And it would bug me. I often felt that maybe he did not approve of me or maybe it was something I did. Maybe my boss was not pleased with my work and minimized interacting with me because of this. And like all things left unclear, what I felt soon became my reality.

It wasn't until I decided to seek clarity on the true status of our relationship that things started to get better. As it turned out, the same feeling that I had was the same feeling that my boss had. My boss felt that I was not fond of him and felt it best to minimize interaction with me and reduce friction. Now isn't that just ridiculous. Two adults believing that they are not in good graces with the other and nothing could be farther from the truth. A total misunderstanding based on assumptions and maintained by belief. What's even more surprising is that we ended up developing a wonderful work relationship where we could speak openly and freely, and more often than others. It just goes to show that our assumptions can do us more injustice than an act of injustice itself.

Now I know it may appear to be appropriate that as a boss, reaching out to your employee to resolve an issue would seem like the best thing to do. And this is true because as a boss, it's their responsibility to look out for the overall wellness of their employees. After all, she is the boss and should lead by example right? But there is nothing that says that as an employee, you cannot approach a boss to speak on an issue. And as you can see from my situation where the employee thought that I did not like her. I didn't even know there was an issue until someone else told me, and this could be the exact same thing that's happening with you and your boss. She may not know there is a problem and you cannot fault her if he does not seek you out to talk about it.

But to provide total clarity, I will tell you my story and why the employee taught that I hated her. And if you could only guess what the issue was. One day I was coming into the building and she said hi to me and I did not respond or acknowledge her. She taught that I was being rude because I was not polite or courteous to acknowledge her greeting and respond. I do not however, recall that situation. If she did say hi, I must have been totally in a different zone, totally distracted or just did not hear her. But for her, the most logical explanation was that I totally ignored her. Imagine if she came to me to get clarification on her assumption that I did not like her. In the end, I did manage to speak to her and we were able to resolve the issue, and chalk it up as a simple miscommunication between us. But I can only imagine how much further and what kind of professional relationship we could have developed, if clarification was sought earlier.

So before you run off with your belief that your boss hates you, consider if you presented any kind of demeanor that would make your boss believe that you are not approachable. Yep it could happen. As a manager, I can certainly say that I have had employees who were not easy to approach and even worse, deal with. And I even have to accept responsibility later on that my fragile relationship with my boss could have spawned from a past interaction with me that made him feel that I was not in favor of him. And it could be the same with you and your boss.

In closing, most bosses do not go out of their way to create poor relationships with their employees and would prefer to fix one than keep it uncertain. And this may seem hard to believe based on what you have heard or experienced, but I can assure you that it's true. So before you make your stance on your position that your boss does not like you; and a position probably lacking both fact and evidence to begin with. Ask your boss if you can speak to him or her and tell them what's wrong. By doing so, you will get the facts and eliminate any assumption that you are not liked. And who knows, maybe it could be the start of a wonderful work relationship. Which I believe will be best for everyone in the end.

My Problems May One Day Make Me Problematic

Ok, so things aren't working the way that you believe it should. Certain aspects about the company bug you and you want to bring to an end. You bring it to the attention of your manager and she speaks to you about it. Your manager was able to resolve the issue, you were satisfied and life goes on.

Not soon after you experience something that you believe you have to bring to the attention of your manager once again. This time, you are right and your manager thanks you for bringing the issue to light. And then another issue comes up. Of course you're going to take it to management because that's what policy states to do. Whatever issue you have you should bring it to management. You're just following the policy.

But you begin to notice that the manager is not as welcoming as the last ten or fifteen times that you spoke with her, and she gives the solution and ends the conversation abruptly. Did you do something wrong by bringing the issues to the manager?

Well frankly yes because too many problems can eventually turn you into a problematic employee. If you ever wanted to know who would be considered a nightmare employee, then become the one that complains the most and you will be that person. Making a complaint is not a bad thing, but complaining about everything can be. Bosses will engage you to discuss a couple issues but they will not be happy with having a discussion about a problem, every time he or she sees you. If there is anyone who knows about problems in a company, it's someone from the leadership or management team. In fact that's part of their job. Solving problems. However, even though it's part of their job it's not necessarily something he or she likes to do. In actuality, bosses don't like problems, they like solutions. So if you are going to pump out an overflow of problems, you should also suggest some solutions as well.

So when it comes to complaining or presenting an issue you should at minimum: try to solve the problem on your own before bringing it to the attention of your manager, evaluate the situation to see if it's something that needs immediate attention or it can wait, offer or suggest an applicable solution to the problem where applicable. If you put some time into resolving a situation on your own, you will find that you are quite capable of doing so. And by the way, before you go to your manager to correct the issue did you stop to think about the possibility of it not being an issue or a relevant one in the first place? Not because something seems wrong does it mean that it is wrong. Not because it seems simple to fix does it mean that it is simple to fix. Not because you believe that you have a solution should you automatically assume that your solution will work. Not because the situation seems like it's something you may not be able to solve, does it means that it is so. And just because a situation seems to be at defcon five, an imminent treat or clear and present danger to you, it does not mean that it's actually an urgent matter. Now it's always better to be safe than sorry, but it's also important to evaluate an issue and gauge it's urgency before you bring it forward. And while your ejecting your plume of complaints and offering your grand solutions, please remember to put some thought into your solutions before you offer them. In other words, don't make your manager have to beef up security and put you under close observation, because of your suggested corrective measures.

But for the sake of clarification please don't think that if you think about the problem hard enough it will go away. The message here is you should give the issue a hard look to see if it's actually an issue. And in doing so, you can save yourself and your boss some unnecessary problem solving time.

As mentioned before bosses don't like problems and especially those that you should be able to fix on your own. And from a boss's perspective, an individual who finds problems with everything is usually concerned only with self. Even if they portray an image that their concerns are for everyone, it's still obvious that it's about self-interest. And even if it were not the case, it's how the boss sees it and this can have a negative impact on your work relationship with your boss.

But don't let this be a reason for you to shy away from presenting an issue or concern to your boss. In fact, not because you have an issue does it mean that you should present it as such. And as you will hear me say over and over, it's not the what, it's the how. What you need to know is although bosses don't generally appreciate problems they very well appreciate lending assistance or giving advice. So by using some tact you can disguise your issues as an informative or advisory meeting and get an opportunity to present your issue. And whenever you solve an issue on your own. Share it with them. Because although they may not like to hear about problems, they certainly don't mind listening to the ones that were solved.

Venting - The Right Way

There are times when we need to let it all out. Sometimes we just had a bad day and need to express how we feel to someone. And this is quite understandable because the workplace can become very stressful. At times, the stress can generate from external factors such as relationships, finances and school which can have an effect on your work performance. But just like all other matter relative to maintaining a professional demeanor, it's not about what is done it's about how it's done.

So now we will examine the fundamentals of properly vending in the workplace because it's not just about letting it out to ease the frustration. It's about going about it the right way, to yield the best outcome. And when I say yield the best outcome, I mean venting in such a way that you will feel good about letting it out, and the possibility of repair for whatever went wrong is high. Very often you will find people channeling their frustrations in the wrong way, which can ultimately leads to further frustration. They have a problem so they decide to tell their best friend or a close working colleague. Sometimes they even go to a chat room and tell everyone in the group what went wrong during the workday. Telling a friend or coworker is one thing, but broadcasting your work frustrations in a chat room is a big NO NO. This is something that a smart professional will never do.

I remember in my early school years there was a problem solving process known as the five W's and it was used to fully comprehend the character, plot and outcome of a story. The same process is also very common in investigative journalism as part of a complete investigation that hits all of the important factors that relate to the story. And it's a simple and effective tool. It simply involves consideration of who, what, when, where, why and if you want to add a bit extra, the how as it relates to what you are trying to find out. The cool thing about the five W's is that you can apply it to almost anything you do. And trust me with the right application it works. And when you apply this process to almost anything you do in the workplace, you show that you can think critically, evaluate situations and make the best decision possible. You will also save yourself a great bit of frustration in the future, by not making any irrational decisions that may affect your job.

So to give you an example of how the five W's and H will work in a venting scenario, we will first structure the best question format for each word. The who represents the person or group you will be venting too. The what represents the issue that you will address or seek to resolve. The when represents the timing and mental status of all involved in the venting session and this includes you, the listener and anyone else who might be involved in your venting session. You have probably heard that there is a time and place for everything and knowing where to vent, especially in a people venting scenario, is absolutely important. The why will cover the benefits or regrets associated with venting. And finally the how will cover the process or format you should take in order to vent. Now please keep in mind that the effectiveness of this process is not based on maintaining a chronological order of who, what when, where, why and how but by understanding and applying the steps appropriately.

So as we begin we can see that the who is pretty self-explanatory. But the right who is also very important. And this is simply because everyone will not treat the information you gave them in the same way. So who exactly should I vent to when I have a problem? Well you should always remember that the most meaningful purpose of your venting should be to find a proper outlet and a solution to the problem if any. And the person receiving your information should be able to assist or at minimum listen attentively and provide support. The person should also be trustworthy with confidentiality or best use of the information they just received about you because if there not, you can run the risk of having your venting session disseminated to other employees. Even worse, through this type of unapproved disclosure of your information, your words could be altered thereby creating new statements of what you said. This is how rumors can start and if it's a very personal matter or a situation that involves another coworker or supervisor, there is a possibility that the other person can get wind of the situation. And the version that they get could be way different or very misleading compared to what you originally said. So the first and most obvious point of relief would be a person in-charge of the employee grievance department if the company has one. If not, then your second option would be someone who can listen to and resolve your issue, and give consideration to confidentiality or best use of your information. This person can be someone in an authoritative position such as a training officer if you're still in training, supervisor, manager or HR supervisor. Now please keep in mind that you could very well have coworkers who are quite capable of providing useful information, assistance and adhering to strict confidentiality or best use of your information. But this is not about what the person can do; this is about you and what you're venting can resolve or potentially make worse. So the folks who are in administrative positions will always be a better selection for you to vent too. And this is not simply because they have administrative positions, but because their administrative positions set certain guidelines for how they handle employee information in terms of confidentiality and best use particles. A manager or supervisor who does not adhere to confidentiality or use your information in an inappropriate manner, can subject themselves and the company to legal issues so they will most likely do the right thing with it.

Now by all means there are some issues that you can discuss with your coworkers, that do not run a significant risk if they decide to share it with others. But you will have to know exactly what you can discuss with them. And what to discuss is also important regardless of whom the listener is, be it a supervisor or a coworker.

As a manager, I have had to deal with employee work related grievances and non-work related personal issues. And at times, I have received more information than I think I should have, that the employee could have omitted and still get his or her point across. But nevertheless, I was able to give advice, help find a solution, or point them in the right direction if I could not resolve the issue.

So now that we have an idea of WHO you should speak to we will now discuss what you should vent about in the work place. And we can divide the issues into two categories, personal issues or work related issues. What you discuss depends on what you feel comfortable speaking about, but please be mindful that not everything that comes to mind should flow through your mouth. And although there is nothing wrong with venting, there are some things you should not vent. At least not in the workplace.

As a general rule, I believe that you should not discuss your personal issues with anyone at work, including your manager or HR supervisor. Unless and only unless, such discussion is related to the possibility of your personal issue affecting your job. Say for example you have a parent, sibling or child to take care of, and there's a possibility that this stressful situation can affect your ability to come to work. Then I would say its fine to have this discussion. Because your personal situation can affect your job, and although your manager or HR supervisor may or may not be able to assist with the home care; they may be able to provide some flexibility with your work schedule and or assignments to help relieve some part of your stress.

Now just as with who and with what, there is a when for venting. And it's not anytime you feel like it. Do not believe that as the person with the issue you can assume the role of victim and demand an audience at any time of your choosing. This will probably make your situation worse and put your character under scrutiny. Knowing when to vent is important and it's not just based on your readiness, but also the people that will be involved during your venting session. Furthermore, do not see this advice as strictly related to work but rather a general practice in your life. If instead of venting through conversation your preferred choice is sporting or leisure activity you still have to take into account the people and events in your life that your activity might affect.

There can be drawbacks such as financial and or relationship issues, during your need to seek relief if you do not take into consideration other relevant matters in your life. And the same applies to the workplace. The people who have to deal with your venting should also be given consideration of their ability to work with you. Is this a good time to speak to my manager or supervisor about this issue? Does this issue need their immediate attention? Is this really an issue that I cannot resolve on my own and do I need to involve someone else? Does my coworker seem like he or she is in a mood to talk right now? Always remember that your venting can have direct or indirect involvement from the people at your job, your family and your friend. So remember to always be conscious of others and when you decided to involve them. When you adhere to this method, you will be in the best position to yield the best results.

So now we will discuss where but before we get into further details, we will make one significant point on where not to vent. So for the sake of your own wellbeing, career development and anything else that you intend to do in life: never, ever, never and in case I did not mention NEVER EVER vent a social media site. And if you do, keep it short, non-descriptive and non-graphic. There is no chance of taking it back - NONE. Once you said it, that's it. This is why I always advise folks to never vent or air it all out in a social media channel. My point here is before you hit that post button think about; who you can potentially offend, who can use what you said against you, who can gain access to what you posted and finally, how can this do more harm to you than good. As I mentioned before, if and when you vent let it be for a good cause and because you want to find a resolve.

Now of course one can say that if I vent in a social media forum, there are several people who will respond with advice or support which can help me get through a rough time. Now this can be true but for your six hundred friends of which; three hundred viewed your post, fifty or so gave a like or thumbs up to your rant, twelve or more commented in support of your rant, six or so lends support and two or three actually give advice but it's nothing that you don't already know. Then there maybe one or two folks who actually give meaningful advice and may also advise in a side-note message that says, "hey call me" or "you should call me before you post something up there". Based on the math that's less than one percent of the people who know you that actually gave meaningful advice. You could have called or messaged them personally if that was the case and leave the other three hundred or more people out of it. As I mentioned before, you never know who can gain access to what you said and just how far what you say can travel.

I can recall an event where an employee who we shall call Bob had some not so choice words to say about me in one of his social media forums. Bob was not happy with a decision I had made to suspend him for a day so he had to put it all out there. Well at least the part that made him seem like the victim and not the events that led up to the suspension; and why would he right. His choice of colorful words could only make one surmise that he was more hateful towards me than the decision I made.

As you just read earlier with the example of the amount of friends, how many liked/gave a thumbs up and how many commented. This was the post that Bob had put out there and the one that I just so happened, was able to view. Now I was not friends with Bob on this social media site and if I was, he definitely dropped me like a hot potato. So I had to have seen what he wrote through someone else's account. And that's exactly what happened. Another employee who was friends with Bob in that particular social media site and who I had a very good work relationship with, decided to show me what was being said about me. Not with any mal-intent, but to give me a heads up on the situation. So one could just imagine the really awkward environment when I saw Bob and we said hi to each other. Whether he meant it or not, it was not a good feeling to know that he held so much animosity towards me and I had to speak to him to clear the air. I asked him if he was ok and I asked him about the recent suspension, and how he felt about it. He said that he understood why he was suspended and he was ok with it. Humm Ok! Clearly not the same as what he had to say in his social media post. I told him about what I saw he posted about me and the first thing he could ask was who showed that to me? I told Bob that it really didn't matter and the only thing that matters was if he truly felt that way about me. Bob said that he was very upset that day and he really wasn't thinking when he posted it. But I don't believe that Bob wasn't thinking. I believe that Bob didn't give consideration to future ill effects of what he put out there, or the consequences of where he was venting. Now I in no way approached Bob to make him feel bad or threatened by what I found out. I used it as a coaching session for Bob to know what he could have done differently and why he should not vent on social media sites because it's never, ever, ever and did I mention NEVER EVER a good idea to do so. Get the picture!

Although Bob and I still tried to maintain a professional work relationship, there was always that uneasy feeling when we spoke. At times, I often asked myself if Bob was being honest when he said he only made those comments because he was upset. I could only imagine how he felt and if he felt uneasy speaking to me. After all, it's very hard to gauge an individual and their demeanor towards you if you created an environment that invites doubt of your genuine goodwill towards them. And me being professional or not, does not provide any confirmation to Bob that yeah, it's no big deal. A one 100% avoidable situation if Bob had given consideration to where he decided to vent.

But nevertheless and exclusive of the results of his actions be it right or wrong, as it relates to his chosen outlet. Bob had every right to vent. There was something that was bothering him and he needed to get it out. And this could also be you and your story. Not necessarily as Bobs' but a situation where you wanted to vent to ease the burden or frustration of the issue. And that's simply what venting is. Creating an outlet. A release of pressure. And we all know what can happen if pressure is not released. Yep you can pop. And usually in an explosive manner. That's why it's important to understand that venting is a good thing. And should be practiced whenever possible to help you find a solution, and take control of your issue before your issue takes control of you. This is the why of venting. A reasonable action to help you get through whatever you're dealing with. Now keep in mind that venting is not always a conversation. It can take the form of an activity such as sports, music, relaxation or any other activity that takes your mind off of the negative memory that you harbor. Keeping your mind active, being involved in activities that you like or reflecting on the issue when you have had a chance to calm down and think logically, can often help in fixing the issue. For instance, I have often found that taking the time to reflect on the issue which is basically a form of internal venting, can often times bring me to a different perspective of what was bugging me in the first place. Or some me-time, dabbling with my tablet and smart phone in an attempt to find new and interesting ways to use them, can help to bring me to a rational state where I can think clearly. Ultimately, if it helps to resolve the issue or give you a different perspective about the issue that is useful and productive, then I say let it out.

So we have so far covered the who, what, when where and why of venting and finally we come to the how. How to vent is simply taking a professional standpoint and making a conscious effort to ensure that when you vent and your chosen method, does not negatively affect your release and your resolve. For example, storming into the manager's office to demand a conversation because you have a grievance will probably do more harm than good to your cause. Even if you are correct or in need of an immediate conversation, your questionable behavior could play a significant role in the outcome. Same adheres to other forms of stress relief activities that you may indulge in. Like for instance, if you like to socialize with a drink as a countermeasure of dealing with a stressful situation; getting pissed drunk and cursing out everyone may bring some relief and pleasure, but the end result could be very devastating, especially if it were to get back to your employer. As mentioned before it's never just the what but always the how when it comes to doing almost anything, and yielding the most favorable results.

So vent when you have to. Find an outlet and release. It can mean the difference in your sanity and your ability to function in the workplace, with your family, friends and the general public. It can sometimes be easier said than done, especially if you are an introvert and you keep things bottled up inside. Now letting it out may not always be a good thing either, but a guided release will always be better than an eruption or an explosion. And as is what we do in life, there are some things we can't take back. Venting does not only have to be a measure to deal with a present situation, it can also help in mitigating or relieving future situations and this is why it's a good thing to do. And if you put some taught into venting the right way, you will always increase your chances of finding the proper channel, and achieving your desired results.

Kids Don't Want To Share The Sandbox

Getting along with others is not always an easy thing. And sometimes people can make it very hard for you by forcing their way upon you. It's their way or the highway so to speak and they often make it very clear from day one. But is this the norm and should you just go with the flow?

Well I can certainly say that there is a good chance that you can encounter a similar situation but I can also say that it is not the norm. It may simply be the cards you were dealt and you end up working with someone or a group of people that are heinously territorial. And any challenge or challenger to their law will be met with swift and severe punishment. Well at least in their minds. But however passive or aggressive the individual or group displays their territorial charge, you should be mindful of the fact that it's more about the long term issues and how they can affect you, and not the degree by which they attempt to make you conform to their way. Even if it may seem harmless or manageable to work with them and doing things their way, you have to be vigilant to ensure that their way is not conflicting with your performance. Because at the end of the day, your performance and your continued employment is the most important aspect of your career. And you should never let anyone jeopardize what's important to you. If their way seems to be conflicting with your performance or can be deemed hazardous to your continued employment: do something about it. And do it quickly. The longer you wait, the more you will be exposed to potential problems and the harder it may be to resolve.

Now it may be wise to approach this kind of situation with caution because some individuals or groups can be extreme territorial, and will go to great lengths to get what they want. And chances are they might very well succeed because of their pass history or seniority. However, you should not conform to their way of doing things simply because it's the way they want it. And your non-acceptance becomes even more significant when their way conflicts with the acceptable procedure set by the company. And why? Because it will not be an acceptable excuse that you were following their lead if something goes wrong. Sure your supervisor or manager may consider that you're new, but it will not grant you any degree of clemency from you being responsible. Especially when you should have known better and you were trained on the proper procedure.

Now making you do things their way will not be the only negative encounter you might face when it comes to working with other employees. Sometimes, your coworkers may not want to share information with you that's necessary for you to perform your task. They may be sketchy with information or hesitant to cooperate or help you. This situation can be just as bad for you as one where you were not doing things by the book, and saying that your coworker is not helpful will not be a valid excuse either. So when faced with this issue, do not risk your performance being viewed as poor and you should seek help immediately.

For any of these situations you should always try to resolve it in an expeditious manner. Especially when it can jeopardize your job or your performance. Even though employees are trained on the right way of doing things, one of the biggest misconceptions of new employees is that they should simply deal with the rules set by the people or group that they started working with. So they decide to simply deal with whatever nonsense or issue that the individual or group puts them through, rather than trying to resolve it. And it's not because they fear the individual or group. But because they fear that they will be proven wrong if they bring it to the attention of a manager, simply because the individual or group has seniority. In addition, they sometimes develop the, I don't want to be a snitch syndrome and I don't want to get anyone in trouble. They stay in the situation until they either become comfortable doing it themselves or the situation resolves itself in one way or another. But this kind of thinking is illogical and it only does more for the other person or group than it does for you anyway. If an employee is doing something wrong and they can get you in trouble, you should tell your supervisor or manager immediately. There is no playing it safe and if you don't say anything, then you are also responsible for the outcome.

In addition, do not have to put up with anyone's bullying, harassing, demeaning behavior or harsh way of communicating to you as a consequence of working with them. No you do not. And you should try to resolve it by being firm and standing your ground; letting the other person or group know, that you will not be subjected to their inappropriate communication and behavior. And if it does not resolve the issue, bring it to the attention of your supervisor or manager immediately. I have a simple quote that I say to people all the time. "you deal with what you put up with". If you let people feel that they can treat you any way they feel, then you deserve to be treated that way. Now I'm not saying that anyone deserves to be treated harshly or unfairly. My message here is don't accept it if you don't want to deal with it. Being subjected to crude and inappropriate behavior and communication from your coworkers creates a very uncomfortable work environment for you. And it won't be long before your performance suffers because this type of work environment is not conducive to performing well. You may try to act as if you are ok with how you are being treated but internally, you will always feel alienated and not want to be in that kind of environment.

Everyone is there at the company for their own benefit. And so are you. You being there is not to make their job easier or conform to their way. You being there is to do your job, help your coworkers perform better where applicable, in-turn help the establishment do its job, and be compensated for your contributions in the end. You are not there to be subjected to anyone's nonsense, or to make their life easier. So their personal agenda of having their way is simply that, their own agenda. And in you knowing this, it should make it that much easier for you to resolve this issue, if ever you come across it.

Dealing With Conflicts

The best way to deal with conflicts is to try your very best to avoid them in the first place. And this is one of those situations where it's easier to do than explain how to do it. And yes folks it's very simple to avoid a conflict.

More often than not, conflicts and disagreements are pointless, harmful if left unresolved and in most cases solvable. But it gets even better. There is an old saying that goes "it takes two to tango". And what it means is that any conflict or argument will require at least two people. The agitator who hopefully is not you, and someone else. Yes, they will actually need your buy in for the conflict to spark and gain momentum to become the hot gossip topic on the job. So always do your best to avoid arguments and conflicts at all cost.

Now beyond the all-out brawl and fist fight that hopefully you will never get yourself into, and would never work out for either employee. Most conflicts are of a verbal or conversation disposition. So developing some political savvy and diplomatic combat skills can help you to evade or resolve most workplace related conflicts. So now we will take a look at some of the skills and tactics you can develop and use, to remain drama and conflict free in the workplace.

Dealing With Conflicts - Neutrality

I have often seen new employees get into situations that they could have avoided or even worse, had nothing to do with them in the first place. As the new kid on the block, there may be instances where conflict can arise in your everyday relations with your peers and or your bosses. Some of these conflicts may be due to your direct or indirect involvement but nevertheless, it is important to know why you should avoid them and how you can avoid them.

One such method is being neutral or adopting a standard of neutrality in the work environment. And what exactly is neutrality? Being neutral is simply not being for or against, associated or disassociated with anything and especially anyone as it relates to the workplace. So let's look at a scenario where there is a group of employees that hate another employee named Bill. They are very verbal about their opinions of Bill and his behavior and performance. They ask you what you think about Bill. Through your own experience with Bill you have witnessed some of his behavioral and performance short comings, and you know that what they are saying about him holds validity. But you reply, "I haven't really observed anything and I'm ok with Bill for the most part" or "I don't really know him that well to know what his short comings are".

In this next scenario a group of employees want to complain to management about the office conditions. They want everyone to send formal letters to management to express their grievances. Although you can agree to see some changes and improvement in the office, you do not feel comfortable with this idea. They ask you to send the letter. You reply "I don't feel comfortable writing the letter, however, if management decides to hold a meeting with staff to discuss the issues I am more than willing to be there".

In both instances you are being neutral. You are not pro Bills behavior and performance is lacking, and you are not pro we need to protest the present work conditions. However, you are not outwardly in protest of their accusations or agendas thereby keeping you quote, unquote, on their team. Neutrality keeps you in the safe zone and can potentially remove any culpability based on guilt by association. And being guilty by association means that you can be accused based on the person or group you associate with.

Being neutral is easy. But it's not just about verbal communication. It's also about you being able to associate with everyone in the company and not just individuals or cliques. Not just the popular folks or the office bad ass. It's everyone. Even Bill who everyone seems to have a problem with. You never can tell when Bill might do the unthinkable and become part of the management team or your boss, so it would be good to know that you never had a problem with him. Being neutral, will also place you in a position to be well informed, trustworthy and distinguishable. You are well informed because you are not restricted to interaction with one person or group. You interact with everyone thereby increasing your exposure to information as it relates to work. You build credibility and trustworthiness with folks simply because you are not seen as discriminative and do not take sides. You are distinguishable because more people know you not because you are popular, but because of your sociable and unbiased demeanor.

Through friendships, we can often feel compelled to support our coworker with their conflicts and grievances at work but in my experience, it is never a wise thing to do. I have often seen good employees through their peer association; find themselves in the black listed and soon to be terminated group because of their interest in their coworkers' conflict. So being neutral will help you to maintain your friendship and also keep you free of guilt by association. It is a proven and effective way to avoid conflict in the work place and when used efficiently, it will do more for you than simply keeping you in the drama free zone.

Dealing With Conflicts - The Battle Not Worth Fighting

I remember one day I took my kids to the park. My girls had asked me if we could play basketball in the morning and I agreed. We decided to play up to 15 points, myself versus the two of them; and twins by the way. Now they are only ten years of age but they take competing very seriously. And I know that they were playing to win. Honestly, I could have beaten them with one arm and one leg, combined with giving them a 14 point advantage. But at the end of the match, they won. They won and they gloated. They let me have it and they were in the zone. They were so happy that when we returned home, they were already planning for the next match.

Now one can argue that I gave them the victory in order to not hurt their feelings and to some extent it's true. And one can further argue that my good intentions can do more harm than good because other competitors may not be as lenient as I was. But overall, my intention was not to deceive but rather to motivate. To make them believe they can win. Now does that mean the next time we played I let them win? Maybe I did, maybe I didn't. But on that day, I let them know it is possible and achievable.

So what is the battle not worth fighting, for each individual it is different but the end result should be one that the result is not worth the effort.

There are three battles I do not fight, the one that I won't win, the one not worth fighting, and the one that the victory can be less rewarding than the defeat.

My story of taking my daughters to the park to play basketball relates to a scenario where the winning is not as fruitful as loosing. If I played hard, I would have won outright and possibly hurt more than my daughters' pride. Through victory, I would have demoralized my daughters' ambition to play basketball and possible ruin the rest of their day. What good would my victory have brought me? So it's the lesson not the story that correlates with the notion of, knowing which fight to fight. Simply put, is this fight worth fighting and is this victory worth achieving.

In the work environment, one such example is you work for a company that does customer surveys and there are cubicles in the office that you and your fellow employee use to call clients. Now the work policy states that no employee is married to a cubicle and it's a first come first served basis. So one day you happen to get the peer rated best cubicle in the office but this cubicle is usually used by let's say Bill. Bill sees you in the cubicle and says you're in my spot. What do you do; option (a) repeat to Bill the company policy about cubicle use which I am almost certain he can quote from back to front and almost certainly, is not his first rodeo with the cubicle wars or option (b), give up the space and deal with this matter in another way and at a different time.

Now let's say you took the fight to bill and you won. The boss got involved and agreed with you and now Bill has to sit and watch you in the cubicle that he occupied for a very long time. It would probably feel good wouldn't it? But let's assume that bill uses that spot not because he just wants it but because he needs it. Suppose Bill has been in that same spot because it is accommodating to a condition or disability that he has and his peers, not necessarily his boss knows about it. How would you feel now? How would you feel if everyone viewed you as being insensitive to Bills problems? I think we can all agree that this is one of those battles where the victory can do more harm than the defeat. As you can see, a victory will not always yield a positive result so it's very important for us to evaluate a situation, before we engage and take a stance.

Now say for example you work for a company that does customer surveys and there are cubicles in the office that you and your fellow employee use to call the clients. Hey I know it's the same example but just keep reading. Now the work policy states that no employee is married to a cubicle and it's a first come first served basis. So one day you happen to get the peer rated best cubicle in the office but this cubicle is usually used by let's say Bill. Bill sees you in the cubicle and says you're in my spot. What do you do; option (a) repeat to Bill the company policy about cubicle use which I am almost certain he can quote from back to front and almost certainly is not his first rodeo with the cubicle wars or option (b) give up the space and deal with this matter in another way and at a different time.

Now if you choose option (a) and win, you may find yourself ascended on the social status ladder as the office badass. The alpha male of the office pack and hey, good for you sport. But if you lose, you can be the laughing stock of the office and another victim of Bill's supremacy, born of his influence and stature amongst his peers and bosses. In my opinion this is a classic case of the battle not worth fighting. This is one of those situations where you could have simply given up the seat and moved to another vacant spot. And with a little investigating and observation, have known that particular spot was a hotbed for controversy. Sure you know the policy and would be correct to stay but what is there to gain from it? Just a work location and it's more than likely no different than the other cubicles. Clearly a conflict that's not worth the hassle.

Now we come to the battle we may not win. And as with our past example, scenario of the cubicle and employee Bill; but this time there are different options. Yes the very same example and yes I did it on purpose. So the boss comes into the office and says to you "I know we have a policy but Bill will use that cubicle, we will speak about it further in a bit" Now clearly the Boss contradicts his policy of first come first serve by giving it to Bill and knowing this do you (a) quote the policy to the boss who could have been influential in writing it or wrote it himself or herself or (b), consider the matter concluded and follow up later. Well my friend if you choose option (a), I hope you have a lot of resources because you may need it to gain victory in this battle. Now it is very clear that you have substantiating evidence that you should have the cubicle but will that be enough to bring you victory in this conflict. But it's the policy right?

Proving the boss and Bill wrong especially in an open public forum and witnessed by the other employees, may do something for your character and give some buy in to a future office badass status. But only providing that you survive long enough and your conflict does not start a chain of events that lead you out the door. And even if you took it higher up and you being armed with policy, there is still a chance it may not end in your favor. If we look at this example we can find some clues that point to why this may be a battle to just let go. As you can see, the boss willingly disregards one of the policies and this should have been a huge red flag that you should evaluate this situation thoroughly before you challenge it. And what boss would jeopardize his or her credibility by contradicting one of their policies unless they had a damn good reason for doing so.

So remember, knowing which battles to fight is extremely important. You must always try to evaluate and be rational about the issue before you decide to make your stand. And finally, no matter how much effort it will take to avoid the conflict, it will ultimately be better than a little effort to attain victory.

Dealing With Conflicts - Put your Pride Aside

I have seen situations where employees who were not the agitator, lose their job because they had to take action right then and there and defend their position. When asked they often mention "well I have a high sense of pride" or "I took offense to what he or she said because it was not true". I will tell you now that pride is a condition that often lands a good employee in a bad situation, because they let their pride guide their actions. Always remember that survival in the workplace is about thought process and strategy - Always! And your pride or sense of pride, can often conflict with your sense of better judgment.

So what exactly is pride? So once again we turn to Webster and his infinite wisdom to ascertain the meaning of the word pride. And according to Webster, pride is described as "a feeling that you respect yourself and deserve to be respected by other people, "a feeling that you are more important or better than other people", and a feeling of happiness that you get when you or someone you know does something good, difficult etc.". At the end of the day, it's simply a feeling. Something that you can suppress or redirect to come to the most logical decision in order to overcome whatever you're dealing with. Now let's whip out that old thesaurus and take a look at the synonyms associated with the word pride.

Self-respect, ego, pride-fullness, self-esteem; all of which can be challenged and in your response to defend your position, make you just as accountable as the agitator. Removing your sense of pride and replacing it with a rational and logical standard to deal with issues will be most beneficial. Remember, your sense of pride is a measurement only you know and display. And what can cause you to have to defend it can be different for me or someone else. For example, whenever dealing with an issue I try not to take things personal. And even if I do, I try my utmost best not to show it. I'm saying this because I am human and will take offense to the statements or actions of others. But I can also apply opposing characteristics and behaviors in order to deal with the offense. There have been instances where I have been verbally attacked by an employee and what was worse, I was their manager. Now I could have taken a stern approach and even charged my employee with insubordination or conduct unbecoming of their expected behavior. However, I took myself out of it, thus removing my feeling of pride and my ego being in jeopardy. If I had to take a stern approach to dealing with the situation, then I would be doing the exact same thing as the other person and enforcing the battle of the egos. To an end and at the cost of either the employees behavior or my credibility as a manager. To further emphasize my point, we will go back to a training session that I conducted with a group of new employees. During the session, I was turning off my phone because it kept ringing, and I was being asked a question by one of the trainees at the same time. The trainee thought that I was not paying attention to the question so the trainee barked at me. "You're not paying attention to me" the trainee said. It was so loud and shocking, that I had to pause for a second. Even the class paused with that uneasy feeling that something really bad was going to come of this for the trainee. I repeated the question that was asked of me back to the recruit and said "I can multitask". I then answered the question and continued as if nothing ever happened. At the end of the training, several trainees came up to me and said that I handled that situation very well. They said that they taught the trainee would have been excused from the rest of the course. Well it just so happened that I had just spoke to the class about how as professionals, we should not take things personal. I also reiterated to them that this was a perfect example of how we should not let our pride get the better of us.

That's what it means to be a professional. Another instructor could have easily dismissed the trainee because frankly, it was a bit humiliating. But because I did not let my pride dictate my actions, I was able to do much more with a negative situation and reinforce a message with the new recruit's. I even had a chance to coach the trainee who said that they felt I was not paying attention to the question. There goes that pride again; dictating the individuals actions and overpowering their sense of evaluation, logic and good judgment. And it will not be satisfied until it feels vindicated. Even worse is when someone is so prideful, that they don't even know what will bring them satisfaction. In fact, the other person's willingness to forfeit and end the issue seems to make matters worse. This is when your pride is really controlling your actions and you don't even realize when you have been championed and your cause won.

So if I don't have pride, what else can I have to feel good about myself? Well humbleness can be a start. Composure, humility etc. are all characteristics you can develop to deal with conflicts and avoid upholding your false sense of pride. In the end, what will you really achieve by defending your position? Can you put it in your pocket? Can you buy something with it? The answer is no. As in my example, I could have easily flexed my administrative muscles and dismiss the trainee in an attempt to defend my ego and pride. But instead I chose a diplomatic and tactful route to deal with the situation, where everyone would walk away with their sense of wellbeing intact. Being humble, showing humility and maintaining composure, is not a form of cowardice or fear as some would think. It's being resourceful, showing tack and emotional control. All of which are some of the strongest characteristics of professionalism, that an individual can attain.

So never let your pride rule you. Instead, you be the ruler of your pride. Know when to turn it on and when to turn it off. It is not the only resource you have when you feel like your credibility is on the line. And if you have been working hard to be an all-round model employee. Then your credibility, value and work ethics may be all you need to defend your position.

Dealing With Conflicts - Involving Others

Now certainly there are times when you try to act like the opposite side of a magnet and do everything in your power to repel yourself from any sort of interaction with the other person. But sadly, and even though you try very hard, this may not always work. And this is quite ok because we may not always be able to resolve every conflict on our own. In this case, you will have to employ some outside assistance and escalate the issue to someone of authority to bring the issue to an abrupt end. And when you are faced with such a dilemma, speed is of utmost importance. The longer you wait, the worse the conflict can get. The main objective here is to bring the issue to an abrupt end. Even if it means you being viewed as scared of the other individual or being known as a tattle tell, it is not of importance to the real priority. And if this stigma is of concern to you, I will advise that you get over it now, because real professionals don't pay any mind to these identity fears. In fact, they laugh at it knowing that it has no place in the professional work environment nor does it hold significance as any form of hindrance to ones aspirations or desires to succeed.

So knowing when to involve others is key in your efforts to finding a resolve to the conflict. And in an order that does not necessarily conform to a system of: you first attempt to resolve on your own, and then seek assistance. Sometimes based on the situation, getting someone involved might be the best solution to the problem. For example, it may be a rowdy coworker or customer and in such a case, your first response should be to get your supervisor, manager or security involved. And you're not getting them involved because you're scared, you're getting them involved because it's the intelligent thing to do. This is one of those situations that you will need to bring to an abrupt end, because it can potentially escalate if you try to resolve it on your own. And the big picture here is that it's not about if you can resolve it, but rather what happens if you fail to resolve it and it escalates into something worse. As mentioned before, getting the supervisor, manager or security staff involved; especially in situation related to safety will be the most practical and sensible approach to resolving the conflict.

So we have concluded our topic on dealing with conflicts. Sometimes we can avoid them by simply not being around it, knowing when to walk away and knowing when silence is best. We even learnt how to deal with them and which ones are not worth your time of day. All in all, conflicts are negative whether we are proven right or wrong and do little for our credibility even if we were victorious in its resolve. And however right or wrong, you should always seek to improve relations with the other individual or group to remove any chance of conflict in the future. Apologize for the issue even if you're right and work towards developing a cooperative and friendly work environment with everyone around you.

I Want To Achieve More -The Ultimate Professional

In this chapter there are certain attributes of a professional we will not be discussing. For instance, we will not discuss the characteristics of the professional and what you will have to do to become one. We will also not overextend this chapter with any basic knowledge such as behavior, communication, doing things by the book etc. What we will look at in particular is the mindset of the professional and other pertinent attributes that he or she must possess. And finally we will make an analysis of the guide I developed for the PRO in the word professional.

The Professional Mind

If I were to tell you that to be a true profession is to develop a structured way of thinking and doings things a certain way, would you agree with me? Do you believe that a professional standard is a process and not intuitive or case by case responses? If I were to tell you that professionalism as a calculated mechanical process can yield better results than just doing things in a certain order would you agree with this?

The truly professional thinker is in a class by his or herself. This individual has learned how to use every particular skill and ability that one can have to its best use, thereby helping to ensure that an efficient and productive standards is always the outcome. He or she has developed true intelligence of best standards and applications, when it comes to just about anything in the workplace environment. And this intelligence can be easily identified in their behaviors, actions and thought processes. They seem to know what to say and what to do at every moment. But this is just superficial, and it only relates to the observed aspect of their work environment intelligence. These individuals also know what not to say and what not to do as well. For every situation, they evaluate the pros and cons prior to taking action to ensure that their actions are applicable and justifiable. They don't just think about now, they incorporate past results and consider future implications that this particular decision can have. And all of this is taking place through a mental mechanical process to derive at the best decision.

I have come to like the phrase "workplace intelligence". It sound like a skill or ability don't you think? And why not? Working and maintaining your employment is not a simple task. Whether you love it or hate it, you have to put some effort into it if you intend to keep it. The only difference being, the amount of effort you have to put into it. Too little, and you find yourself at the bottom end of the spectrum, probably in a lot of trouble and trying to recover. Too much, and you can find yourself feeling overworked and burnt out. Applying the appropriate professional standard by devolving workplace intelligence, will help you to find that balance. But what exactly is workplace intelligence? Is it knowing everything about the job? Is it knowing how things are done? Well let's bisect the phrase and get to the root meaning to find out.

It is safe to say that we probably don't have to go to Webster to find out the meaning of the word workplace. It's simply the place or environment that we work or any other factors that relate to the job. But I will go to Webster for the meaning of the word intelligence so that we can really drive the message home. So this is what Webster online version had to say. Intelligence is defined as "the ability to learn or understand or to deal with new or trying situations: reason; also: the skilled use of reason: the ability to apply knowledge to manipulate one's environment or to think abstractly as measured by objective criteria (as tests)". All of this is a definition of intelligence but I like to use my own and I will also show you how I apply it to the work environment. Now to the scholars reading my book, please do not think that I am in anyway trying to discredit anyone's work. I am simply trying to give a definition of intelligence that shows format and illustrates a simplified definition.

Intelligence is a four part process made up of four components. And the four components are knowledge, understanding, application and finally best use functionality.

Having knowledge is to know. You know of something. A drinking cup. So you go beyond and you have understanding of how the cup is used. It used to hold liquids. And yes it can hold other things as well but we will keep it simple for now. But what about its application? Can you put it to use? Sure you can drink from it but is that the only use for the cup? The applicable uses of the cup can go as far as your imagination takes it. Have you ever watched a show or read a magazine on how people use ordinary household items to create works of arts or other practical items. Or you have seen a show about outside survival, and the person or group would take whatever they could find and put it to good use. Some of it can even be lifesaving essentials but before it was needed for that purpose, it was considered junk. This is what I mean by best use functionality as the last component and deciding factor of intelligence.

For most people the basis of intelligence stops at application. Someone knows, they understand and they apply these factors to come to a conclusion. Now don't get me wrong, there is nothing wrong with this approach and you can still come up with good results. But when you apply best use functionality you take your intelligence to a higher level. This is true intelligence. Refined intelligence.

I have often had debates with friends, family and coworkers on intelligence and how my viewpoint relates to a scenario where someone is deemed intelligent. The conversation goes like this "he is a really intelligent guy but he always finds himself in trouble". I would counter that statement with if he is so intelligent, why hasn't he not come to the conclusion that being in trouble is not a good thing and he should use his intelligence to stay out of trouble. I say, he may be knowledgeable, he may understand, but his application of what he knows is not for best use. In the end, it does him more harm than good.

Didn't Webster say that intelligence is the skilled use of reason: the ability to apply knowledge to manipulate one's environment? Where is the intelligence if at the end of it all, your intelligence gets you nowhere? And if we combine the words workplace intelligence we can see it's meaning in its entirety. Workplace intelligence is the ability to use every aspect of the job, which also includes the people the environment and the applicable factors to find the best use application. This is what you will need to develop. This is what will make the difference in your day. And this is the distinguishing characteristic of a true professional.

Intelligence specifics for the work environment. Wow, that's huge. Sure makes me feel good every time I say it. But is best use application of what I know and have at my disposal the most I can get out of my efforts? If you're doing it only for your own benefit then that's all there is to it. But if you are considering the rest of your coworkers and the institution as beneficiaries of your efforts, then we can add something else to the process.

Reasoning

So not that we know the mindset of the professional how does this person apply what they know and understand about their job? In other words, what's their reasoning or logic involved in the way they do things? What will be the benefit of thinking a certain way?

Welcome to the world of the big picture thinker. He or she is that individual who puts every thought, every action into consideration of how the results will not just benefit self, but their job, their coworkers and the institution. To the big picture thinker, it's not about me. It's not about my ego or my pride. It's about the achievement for all of us. Even if at my expense: if it benefit's the majority, then it's the best outcome. Some people may find this advice hard to accept and will not budge on their position to receive their just deserts. But unknowing to such individuals, there can be benefit's to every defeat. And on the same token, there can be losses incurred to every victory. It's the "what if" parameter that guides the action in anticipation of the result. It's looking at where ten possible steps can take you before you make the initial first step. Remember in the chapter dedicated to dealing with conflicts we spoke about the battles worth not fighting. The ones you will not win, the ones not worth fighting and the ones where the victory can be worse than the defeat. These are all traits of a workplace intelligent, big picture thinking professional. Imagine a scenario where you and one of your coworkers are meeting with your manager to discuss an issue between the two of you. At the end of the discussion you are proven right but instead of basking in your victory, you offer it up in an effort to resolve the conflict in its entirety. You say to the individual. "Hey I would like to apologize for the issue we had between us. If we can continue working together I'm very much ok with that and look forward to working with you again. At the end of the day I'm a team player and I will do what's necessary so we can continue working together and leave this issue behind us". Wow, that would be a huge seller of your communication, people and conflict resolution skills. The manager might be so impressed that she may say to herself, "I can retire sooner that I thought now that I found my replacement".

Workplace intelligence and being a big picture thinker will form the basis for your ability to think critically and logically. When you start thinking critically and logically, you remove the debris and other forms of distortion that misleads your sense of better judgment or reasoning. For example, someone says something about you and you take it personal. Now I know this has been overkill because you have heard me say it a thousand times but for the sake of driving the point home, I will say it one more time. You should never take things personal. Professionals don't, or at least they have become very skilled at not showing it. If you take it personal, you put yourself at the center of the issue and self-preservation will most likely win over best decision and any chance of rational or logical thinking.

Another example is your ability to handle criticism. You are criticized for your performance and you explode because you put so much effort into what you did, and it's still not good enough. As a professional, you take criticism for what it worth. You are being critiqued. When not in professional mode, you can explode because you believe it was a personal attack against you. What you should do is listen and evaluate what is being told to you. After taking some time to evaluate what was said, then you present your response in a calm controlled format. And what do we call this. It's called emotional control.

For most people and most situations, emotion control means not getting upset. But in the work environment, emotional control should mean, knowing when to use the right emotion at the right time. It's not about stifling an emotion; it's about portraying the most applicable one. For example, have you ever been somewhere that you just don't want to be and as the saying goes, it's written all over your face? Now surely you can be upset about where you are, but does that mean that everyone has to know? I'm almost certain that with ten minutes of emotional control and portraying a sense of wanting to be there, leaving soon after will go over way better than leaving at the end and your interaction said you did not want to be there at all.

As a true professional, part of what you do is doing your best. And you don't do your best because of a reward or for recognition. You do your best because you believe in the quality of your work and the value that is inherent in striving to do your best. There is an old saying – "practice makes permanent" and the more you try to perform at your best the faster you will develop the discipline to always do your best. Always remember that your standards are the outcome of what you put into yourself, so why not ensure that you are the greatest beneficiary of your efforts. And doing you best also involves not taking shortcuts. And don't take this literally to mean that as a professional, you will always work through the process from A to Z and not ever miss a single step.

What I am saying here is to avoid short cuts that take away from the quality of your results. When YOU know that the outcome is not as it should be even if everyone else thinks that it is, as a professional this should bother you. For example, if you work at a restaurant and you are tired, and the last burger fell on the floor. Don't serve it to someone because you are tired. Sure they may not know, but YOU will know. This is where you must always exhibit proper ethical behavior. It's like someone asking you if you always follow proper table manners. And you say yes. Well, unless you eat with a knife, fork and a napkin every time, and not just when in the presence of others, then you don't always practice proper table etiquette.

In addition, did you know that true professionals do not see problems? Ok that may be a stretch but they do their best to minimize the viewpoint that they have a problem. Or tackle the situation as if there was never a problem in the first place. Sure they may be petrified and scared as hell, but they know that it has to be resolved anyway. Problems only exist because of our inability to solve them or prevent them. So you don't look at anything as a problem of issue. All you see is an event that you need to deal with. If you think that doing your job is a problem then all you will do is have problems. And it would probably work in your favor if you have some sense of optimism because I can only imagine the nightmare mindset of an individual whose job it is to solve problems, and they themselves are of a pessimistic disposition by nature. Talk about hell on earth. And being optimistic is not being unrealistic and a positive Polly, with no sense of realism that the results cannot always be as desired. It's just tackling a problem with a positive outlook first and not dooming your outcome before you even start. You know, not being a negative Nancy and throwing in the towel: essentially giving up before you gave it your best shot.

Remember in earlier chapters we spoke about the reality of perception and how it affects you in the workplace. Well what good is all of this if you're not keeping a personal score card on how you are doing or what you need to improve. As a professional, it would be a good idea to solicit feedback from the people you work with directly and indirectly. Direct involvement being your coworkers, bosses and indirect, being clients and customers. You can think that you are doing great but it does not mean that you are. Remember the big picture thinker approach is how your efforts can benefit all and not just yourself, so feedback would definitely aid in recognizing your good and not so good performance.

So not that we understand the mindset and reasoning of the professional, we will take a look at a simple process that a professional should use that will fully enhance and compliment his or her mindset to provide the best results. The procedure is called the think PRO approach to dealing with everything in the work environment. Whether you are solving a problem, giving advice or completing a task, this procedure will help to ensure that you maintain best practices and best use application. The PRO stands for Procedure, Resources and Outcome. Procedure is basically the formal way of doing things as set by your rules, regulations, P&P and anything else that provides a description on what your job is and how it should be done. A professional also has built in procedural standards and stays within these parameters when doing their job. Your mindset and reasoning standards must work in cohesion with procedure in order to maximize on the best possible output. Resources are anything at your disposal that you can use to provide the best outcome and the most benefit to all involved. However, resources must always be in accordance with what's at your disposal and not what you would like to achieve. They must also coincide with the procedural aspect of you job and your expectations. The only exception being when you position or job role gives you the flexibility to manipulate, add or change resources to achieve the desired outcome. And even on this level, you should minimize the level of deviation from procedure for the sake of gaining resources. And to sum this up into one simple explanation. Never let your ambitions outweigh your resources. Don't let the intended outcome be it beneficial or not, make you seek out resources that you do not have or use resources that you do not possess to achieve your goal.

We now come to the outcome section of think PRO. Your outcome or result is equally as important as the effort you put into it. So working hard and not seeking the best outcome is doing yourself an injustice. Your outcome should serve as your measurement standard to gauge where your efforts are and where you can make improvements. And it's not about your doing it bad but rather, about seeing how you can do it better. As a true professional, refining your efforts to improve your outcome will help to keep you focused on the meaningful aspects of your job, your performance and a contribution that benefit's all.

Make Yourself Known

Have your ever heard someone say "hiding in plain sight". It means that you're right in everyone's face and no one can see you. When it comes to anything that involves the institution, there is nothing worse than an invisible employee. And when it comes to the individual, there is nothing worse than being the invisible employee. Because being visible or invisible, can make the difference in your success and your failure in your efforts to excel.

So who exactly should we characterize as an invisible employee? Well it's any employee who remains in shadow. Any employee who keeps to themselves, limiting their level of socialization and communication with others. The employee who limit's any opportunity to gain any kind of distinguishable characteristic and as a result, hides in the open.

We can even have several distinguishable features that give us identity but we can still be invisible. And it's not just descriptive characteristics that make someone invisible. I can know your name, your face and other identifiable features about you, and you can still be invisible to me.

Sadly, most folks assume that visibility in the workplace is a descriptive disposition. Some people also believe that because they have distinguishable characteristics, it can suffice as their ability to be noticed. The really buffed guy. The really pretty girl or the tattooed girl or guy. Or the really weird name that's hard to pronounce. Now in some cases it can as in the guy with the orange hairstyle. What are the odds of two people with orange hair working in the same department or for that matter the same company? Or your name being Seymour Butts. Say it a couple times you'll get it. And if this happens to be your name I apologize in advance but overall you see my point. These descriptive characteristics can certainly make you easily identifiable amongst the crowd but visibility requires more from you.

An employee is invisible when he or she through limited interaction and communication, cannot be easily identified for who they are. As mentioned before, I can know your name, face and your orange hair style, but I still do not know anything about you. And why is this so? It's so because the most important part of your identity in the workplace is your contribution. That's right, your contribution and how you go about letting everyone know who you are and what you can offer to the establishment. What you do, how you do it, when you do it and why you do it. And to top it all off, what else you intend to do. When the people in your company get to know you in this way, it is then you become visible.

You can be a great employee and you can be a significant contributor to the establishment. You can also harbor enormous potential to grow and further contribute to the institution. And for what's it worth, you can have all of these positives and no one knows about it.

This is the consequence of you being an invisible employee. All of your efforts, all of your contributions, your ideas, dedication, everything: all of it, unnoticed. Imagine a politician running for office and cannot prove their worth. Would you vote for this person? A name just pops up out of nowhere and is running for office. Wow, good luck with that. Their chances of success will be slim to none. And you my friend are no different to a politician. You will have to campaign yourself if you want to gain recognition and avoid being invisible.

Now as we have read, being invisible can cause your efforts to go unnoticed but what about the effects? When you're invisible every ounce of your dedication, effort and contribution becomes undervalued. And be mindful that I said undervalued. You work extra hard, you show the highest degree of loyalty, and you have so much to offer. But the only one who knows this is you. Ok, maybe your immediate supervisor and some of your colleagues know but is it enough to bring light to your overall performance? Sure you may gain some momentum but this may not be enough if you want to really gain recognition.

Relying on a few people and what they know about you as a tool to disseminate good information about you is not a reliable strategy. If you want your contributions and any other good quality about you to gain recognition, you will have to do it yourself. Sure your supervisor may speak highly about you but what guarantee is there it will get to the people who need to hear it? And besides, you're not the only one who they may be speaking highly of if you work in a company with hundreds of employees. Also, your coworkers may say good things about you but the reach of their influence may be limited. Or better yet, they may not say anything at all because in the end, they want to move up as well. And you can't be upset at them because it's only natural for people to want for themselves before others. Remember the workplace is a competitive environment and your success will rely on your efforts.

And what about customers and clients? Sure they may tell you that you are wonderful but that's only of value to your personal growth and self-esteem. If no one else knows about it, it doesn't exist or never happened. And getting this information out there is a great performance validator. Now there are some companies that do not encourage their employees to solicit feedback but in general most companies do. And if your company does, spare no effort in having those satisfied customers and clients advocate on behalf of your performance. This is a huge seller of your performance because it is unbiased and the customers and clients can only be motivated by the satisfaction of their experience with you and the service you provided.

So now that you know the importance of making yourself know and the fact that it's up to you to do so, we will now discuss what you should be known for. You should always strive to be known for everything positive and nothing negative. And even if you experience negative, you should be known for handling and dealing with the situation in a positive manner. Positive in this case being in an adult, professional manner. And this should always be your goal. To be viewed in a positive light.

Now here are some qualities and attributes you should be known for. And to keep things organized, we will place them into two groups. One being personal and the other work and people related.

Personal attributes and qualities will include- being dependable, being trustworthy, honest, and loyal and a sense of happiness in the work place. And if I had to pick one, I would say you should always be known for being happy at work. Because if you're not you can make every other quality seem false.

And as far as work and people related qualities. Well those would include-being sociable, being a team player, problem solver, a joy bringer, being a neutral and unbiased thinker, and finally a model employee. And if I had to choose one of these qualities, I would pick being sociable as the number one quality you should possess. Being able to approach people and being approachable will be necessary if you want to develop any of the other qualities. And since you will have to do most of your campaigning yourself, I suggest that you work on being personable as soon as possible.

In the end if you want to grow you have to make yourself, your efforts and your contributions known to the people in the organization. Even recognition from a bad experience can do more for your career than not being recognized at all. Achieving your dot on the map and letting everyone know you are in the game is a necessary step towards the achievement of your goals.

Avoiding Errors

Most people do not go out of their way to make mistakes. In fact, most work related errors are either due to not being aware of the consequences, or not fully thinking things through. But in reality, making a mistake should be something that you make an effort to avoid at all cost. The fact is that mistakes can cost you, your team and the institution so as an employee; you should never look at a mistake whether big or small as nothing to worry about.

Let's say for instance you work for a cab company. And one day you had a small accident. Although it's a small accident this is still a big deal. Any why, because for you it may be a small accident costing the company a couple hundred bucks to repair. But when these small accidents build up, it can run into the hundreds of thousands of dollars in expenses for the company. And cost is not only associated with a monitory loss. There is also cost in time and effort to complete the investigation, and to conclude this matter. So a small matter to you can be detrimental from a global perspective to the business. Errors will also affect the level of confidence that your clients and customers have in your goods or services. Let's say for example that you and your friends buy coffee from the same diner, and the waiter always seem to get your order wrong. Eventually, you may stop buying from them right? You may also express your displeasure to your friends who may also stop purchasing from the diner. And with enough mistakes, the diner can lose credibility in its service and send its customers elsewhere. So in knowing that errors and mistakes on your part are more than just your issue, you should make every effort to avoid them.

So how do you avoid errors? Well as humans to say that we can always avoid errors is being superficial in thought and ludicrous in expectations. But you can still make a conscious effort in trying to be error free in order to minimize the possibilities.

So the first thing you should always do is keep your wits about you and stay focused on your task at hand. Sticking to procedure and maintaining acuity to the task from beginning to end, will help to minimize the possibility of error. When we sway from procedure and task focus, we open Pandora's Box to a world of possibilities related to mistakes. You can be on your a-game for twenty years and the one day on work you decide to take it easy, you suffer the biggest disaster of your career.

Task preparedness and readiness will also play a significant role in you minimizing errors at work. Taking a responsible approach to ensuring that you are prepared for work will help to ensure that your duties go error free. And as logical and straightforward as this might seem, I have often had to coach employees on the importance of coming to work prepared and in a manner fit for duty. I'm sure we have all heard stories of company vehicle crashes and accidents, and when the employee is screened to assess their state at the time of the incident, they were not fit for duty. Some of these accidents were caused by the employee being intoxicated. Others were caused by the employee being tired and fell asleep at the wheel. These are all inexcusable errors and show a lack of better judgment and professionalism. A responsible employee knows that he or she should not go to work right after partying, tired and hung-over. Or even worse, intoxicated. Getting enough rest and allowing enough time to recover from drinking is something that should be considered before you decide to go out partying and drinking in the first place. And if you ever have to give one priority over the other, I can only hope that you choose your job over a hangout. And when you are responsible and plan properly, there is no need for you to have to choose. And it matters not if you are working in the safety department at the nuclear power plant or a pet groomer. It has nothing to do with the type of job you do so tasks do not merit level of responsibility.

These are all examples of situations where people did not put enough thought into their actions and did not think things through. As a professional thinker, your mind is working twenty four seven to make sure that you make the best decision possible. Just because I'm involved in safety should it mean that the person involved in pet grooming, should use less mental muscle in their everyday tasks and don't make safety a concern. It is the mindset of the individual not the task or responsibility that paves the way to a desired outcome.

Another way you can aide yourself in minimizing errors is to never take shortcuts. Now by all means if you know how to shorten the time or effort to complete a task while maintaining the desired outcome, then please do so wherever applicable. There is nothing wrong with being efficient. But if shortening time and effort will result in a lesser or undesirable result then you are simply asking for trouble and deserving of whatever comes your way. The true mark of a professional will be your ability to complete your task to the best of your ability every time.

Every mistake has a consequence and none can be graver that those that breach safety. It's unfathomable to think of the destruction that a train can cause if the driver were to fall asleep at the wheel. Or a pilot who was intoxicated and piloting an airplane with passengers on board. These mistakes can be so severe, that the respective agencies have many processes in place to assist their employees with minimizing these kinds of mistakes at all cost. I cannot stress the importance of adherence to safety standards and never taking shortcuts just to complete a task. This is where your mistakes can have long term consequences for you, the institution, customers, clients and the general public depending on the severity of your error. So always think safety first and ensure that you are mentally and physically prepared to tackle your task, and avoid errors.

But for every effort we make to avoid a mistake they can still happen. And when they do, you must always own up to it. Trying to pass the buck or share blame with someone or something does not remove the error or make it less critical. In fact, it can only make matters worse for you. Now if you are truly not at fault don't say you are guilty and claim responsibility. But know that at fault or not, you were involved in an error and you need to know what you can do if anything, to avoid repeating the mistake. Say for example you work as a two person team in security. Your partner has a habit of falling asleep and one night the place is vandalized and robbed. Now it didn't happen because of you but it did happened to your team. Your goal should be to not only avoid mistakes for yourself, but the team as well. So if you end up getting another partner who has a habit of falling asleep, what should you do? Do nothing, or what's necessary to ensure that the team is successful?

Finally when you're wrong and you know you are; apologize. And when you apologize, mean it. Make every effort to ensure that you do not make the same mistake again because every time you do, you are showing that you did not improve or to some people you do not care. Any of which can have a negative impact on your career and potentially place you employment in jeopardy.

Recovering From A Negative Experience

We have all probably heard the saying "to err is human". But mistakes are not always such a simple thing, and we often have to have had the experience to know how someone will handle a particular error. And sometimes, some of these errors can be so bad that it makes the individual feel like giving up. Sometimes this feeling can last for such a long time that the individual can seem to have changed and this change is usually for the worst.

But left unchanged, these individuals may end up giving up on any possibility to advance in their career. And not necessarily because the mistake is preventing them from the companies perspective, but because they either never found a way to get over the issue, or they make the issue control their future actions by being doubtful or cautious.

Making a recovery to your former self can be difficult at times and this can be very hard depending on what happened. But there is a positive in every negative and a negative in every positive. As a manager, I have counseled many employees on the advantages of a negative experience. Some have used my advice and was able to put their negative experience to good use. Others just took it for what it was, advice, and continued about their business. And if you're wondering what I told my employees was so beneficial about making a mistake, well here it is.

A mistake can be an unforeseen blessing in disguise. Now please be mindful that not all mistakes are the same and some will have graver consequences than others. But if it's one for which you can receive leniency and forgiveness, then you are poised at a point where you can benefit from the mistake. And here's how. Any kind of mistake you make in the workplace will usually be followed up by a formal investigation and remediation. This error has just given you recognition, and a chance to make a good impression. Huh? You might be probably asking yourself right now but yes, your mistake can be an opportunity to make a good impression. Remember in an earlier chapter we mentioned that being know for a mistake is better than not being known for anything at all. Well a mistake although a bad thing, still put you on the map and gives you recognition. But there are some steps you must take in order to make this unpleasant circumstance a blessing in disguise.

So the first thing you must do is accept responsibility. This is your mess up so you must own it. If there is any repercussion for your error then you must accept it. When your supervisor sees that you are taking responsibility for your error she will be more flexible to minimize or even dismiss any repercussion for your actions. The way you respond to an issue the first time will have some influence on any further issue you may have, so it's best to leave a good impression on how you handle these things the first time.

Secondly, if your error is not so egregious that you get to keep your job, don't be afraid to speak about it with others and especially the supervisor or manager who investigated the incident. This is an admirable and adult like character that shows you are confident enough to speak on it. Let them know that you have learned from the mistake and what you are doing to improve yourself. The third thing you will do is not use the issue to punish yourself. Especially if you were reprimanded in anyway for making the mistake. Yes you can feel down because you always like to do a good job, but punishing yourself can make things worse. After a while, you may become so cautious in an effort to prevent a repeat of what happened that you inadvertently punish yourself even more. And there is nothing worse than a feeling that you have to walk on eggshells at your job, which means, that you have to be cautious with everything you do in fear of losing your job.

If you let a negative experience dictate the future of your employment you will not be able to reach your fullest potential. And sometimes people are so entrapped by their errors that they never recover at all. What you will need to do is embrace the situation and see what you can do to make it work in your favor. Don't carry it on your shoulders as dead weight but rather see it as spare parts. Instead, think of it as a Lego set that didn't work out as planned. Now you have extra pieces that if you use properly, can make your next attempt at building and growing more successful.

Becoming An Asset

Are you an asset? Ask any employee at any company and almost all would say that they are an asset to their establishment. And in truth, they are all probably correct. In general, companies are not in the business of incurring expenses unnecessarily, especially if it's an employee who gets paid to do nothing. Ok, except for that one person that you know and you're saying, this writer does not know what he's talking about. So the real question is; not if you're an asset, but rather, how much of an asset are you to the company? In essence, how valuable are you to the establishment.

Now if you were to ask the same employees if their company closed down and their employer opened another company, would their employer rehire them? Most of them would probably say yes. Now ask them if there were a few vacant positions would their former employer hire them? Once again, the majority would probably say yes. Now ask them, if there was only one position would their former employer choose them over everyone else and why? The scary truth is not that everyone would say yes, but rather a great amount would believe that they would be chosen and have valid reasons for believing so. And the fact of the matter is a lot of them could be right and an equal amount of them could be wrong. Where you want to be is in that group of people that believe they are an asset to their company and they really are.

You are probably asking yourself if I just joined the company or haven't been hired yet, how much of an asset am I? And the answer is, if you fill a role in the company you are an asset. But simply being an asset is not enough to secure your position in the establishment because assets do not have the same value. And by value I mean what's your overall worth to the company. Are you that well-rounded and highly valuable employee?

As a newbie, you are most likely lacking the corruptive and negative attributes that experience and seniority can sometimes bring so chances are, you can be molded into the perfect employee. The perfect employee is the type that mirrors the core values, objectives and ideals of the company. So for you it's how do I get there, how do I become more than an asset, how do I become a valuable employee.

There are many attributes an employee would need to be considered valuable. But as a general rule any attribute that you possess must correlate with the three major components of the job; your peers, your bosses and the institution. Your peers must see you as an invaluable part of the work environment. Your boss or bosses must believe you are an asset and also see you as invaluable to the company. And finally, your contribution to the establishment should have a positive and substantial impact. Now keep in mind that your ability to work and complete tasks are also important factors in developing positive work relationships. But these abilities are on a personal level, and may not always contribute to the collective productivity of the team or considered a substantial contribution to the establishment. It is more important or of greater significance if your contribution benefit's the team collectively and generates positive recognition throughout. For example, you will come across workers who simply just do their job. Although this type of worker may complete tasks and assignments necessary in meeting the organizations level of productivity, their contribution may not foster growth and development amongst their peers.

Take our fictional characters who we shall call Tom and Mary. Tom works from 9 to 5 and Tom is able to complete his assignments and tasks throughout the day. What Tom does not do is anything that he believes does not relate to him or his tasks. So when Tom sees Mary doing a task that she is struggling with, he turns a blind eye towards her. Even more disappointing is that the task Mary is failing at could have been one that Tom had done before, and he knows how to complete in a timely manner. As far as Tom is concerned, that's not his problem and Mary will find a way to complete her task or deal with the consequences.

Now let's go back a few paragraphs and ask Tom the same question in relation to being an asset. So we asks Tom, are you an asset to your establishment and his reply is yes. So is Tom right or wrong? Since Tom does his job and the organization requires his service to effectively conduct business, then the answer is he's correct. So we skip through the questions of being rehired and a few vacancies because Toms answers would most likely be yes to the main question. And we ask Tom, if there was one opening would the boss choose you and why? And Tom's answer, most likely being yes, may also be justified by his belief in his work performance and relative to the completion of his tasks and assignments.

But unknowing to Tom, his self-evaluation of his worth to the company will not be the deciding factor in him being rehired. It is the bosses' viewpoint and at times the viewpoint of Tom's peers that will decide his faith. Also, consideration will be given to his contribution to the establishment and its significance if any.

Although Tom's ability to complete tasks and assignments may be an admirable trait, it may not be sufficient to convince the boss that he is the ideal candidate for the position. The boss may also value the thoughts and opinions of Tom's peers. If the collective belief of Tom's peers is that he is not a team player, or his contributions are not relative to the teams' development, this will certainly be a negative aspect of his performance. Coupled with work contribution that is not substantial. Tom may find his chance of filling that one vacant spot to be a lost cause.

So where did Tom go wrong you might ask? And the answer to that is Tom neglected his organizational obligation to his peers and a higher level of performance and commitment to his establishment. Tom was efficient at doing his job but made very little contribution to the institution fulfilling its goal. By not just focusing on his tasks and wanting to do more. And in addition to helping out his fellow employees. Tom would have fulfilled his organizational obligation and gained valuable recognition, beyond his tasks and assignments. By his performance, Tom clearly shows that he is indeed an asset. But his contribution to his teammates and the establishment is not enough to propel him to a status of being truly valuable to the establishment.

Tom's experience also reveals that it is equally as important what people think about us as what we think about ourselves. And loosing value may not be the only misfortune that Tom will experience during his employment. Tom may also diminish his opportunity for advancement or his ability to develop support from the people who he will lead. And if he succeeds in being promoted, Tom will have a tough time inspiring confidence and support from his team. Basically, unless Tom is put in charge of an entirely new group of people, it may be very difficult to lead the same people that he worked with. And why? Because the people who tom did not support will be the same people that he needs support from. And why should they be willing to work with and support an individual who they know did not do the same for them. Even if Tom's position gives him instructional authority over his subordinates and they have to follow his directive, it still will not be easy for him. They will probably just do what they have to do and nothing else. Just like Tom did. And this is the reason why his task of leadership may be difficult. Tom not being the supportive employee to his peers will only help to ensure that he creates a not supportive environment for himself.

So as I mentioned earlier, it will take more than your belief in yourself that you are more than an asset, for you to actually be one. The buy-in of your bosses and your peers will be significant and can often be the deciding factor when measuring your true worth. So if you want to be one of those people who believe you are valuable and you really are; then start working on your positive relationships with the people at your job, and ensure that your contributions go beyond the completion of your tasks.

How To Become Valuable

To be valuable, you will have to appeal to the three most important aspects of the standard work environment, your peers, boss or bosses, and a substantial contribution to the establishment. In past chapters we discussed the attributes needed to be considered an asset or being valuable to an establishment. We also talked about our fictional employee Tom and the reason why it may be difficult for him to lead his team if chosen for a position. We also spoke about another fictional employee named Mary. And as you can recall, Mary was struggling with completing her tasks and this may impact her ability to be chosen if she were also considered for a position. But as we mentioned earlier, our ability to complete our tasks is a beneficial ability that we possess, but it is not the definitive element of being a valuable employee. Now let's say that Mary does not possess the skills to complete her tasks and assignments in an expeditious manner like Tom does. Do you think that she would be less favored to fill a position? If your answer is no, then you're right. Mary may not be able to work as effectively as Tom, but she may possess other positive attributes that make her a better choice than Tom. Suppose Mary had a great rapport with her peers, is considered a valuable member of the team and goes above and beyond to help others. And although she may not be able to complete her tasks as efficiently as Tom, she often does more than is required of her, thus the end result is a substantial contribution to her team and the company. And that's simply what a substantial contribution is. A contribution that involves doing more than just your job. It is a noticeable contribution beyond your tasks and assignments specifics. And your substantial contribution also relates to the effort you make to foster growth and development of the team. So with these factors in favor of Mary, do you believe there is a possibility of her being chosen over Tom? I for one certainly do, and it's due to her encompassing more of the essential elements of being valuable. The diagram below shows the necessary criteria and pathways to becoming an asset to an establishment.

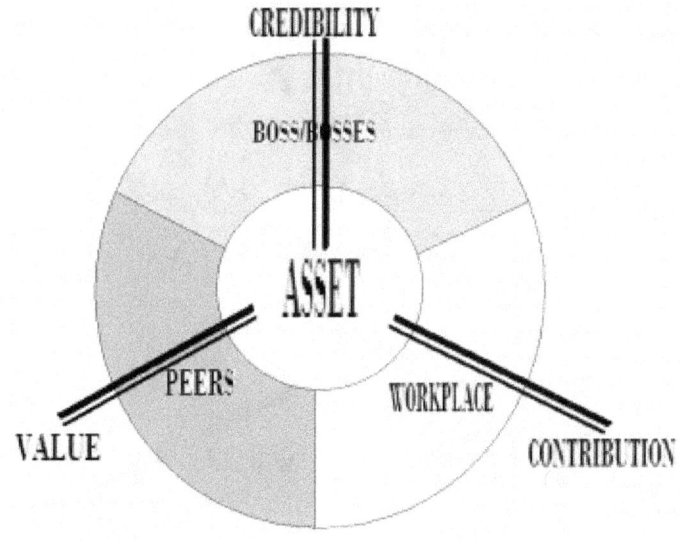

So on the above chart; if we were to use two lines of different thickness to represent the positive effect that an employee has in the work environment, and the thicker line representing a greater or significant impact, what would be the results for Tom and Mary. And while I'm sure that you are sitting there marveling at my extraordinary work of art and its vivid and rich details, there is much more that we have to cover so please keep reading.

Now let's take a look at Toms chart.

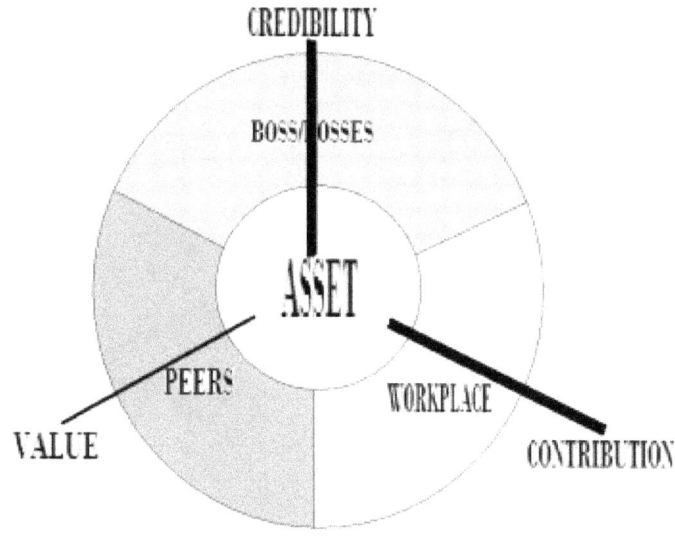

From all appearances and from Tom's point of view, he does his job and he has developed credibility with his Boss so he is an ideal candidate for the position. But what about his peers? Is Tom a team player? Also, is his contribution to the establishment as significant as he believes? Remember it's not your viewpoint of your contribution but the viewpoint of your boss and peers that matters. Now assuming that Tom's boss takes into account the perception of Tom by his peers; if Tom is portrayed as not being a team player or unsupportive to his team, then that would cause a significant impact on his credibility. Also, if the boss does not see his contribution as being substantial, then his chances of being selected will decrease even more. And there is no such thing as; because you are good at doing your tasks, does it mean that you will make a good leader. Leadership involves more than your ability to do your tasks and you cannot lead people by simply giving out instructions.

So in actuality this is what Tom's chart most likely looks like.

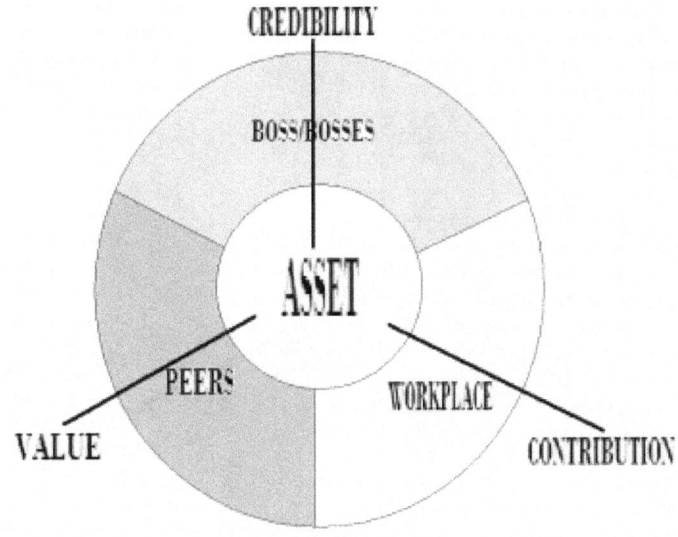

Although Tom may think that his contributions are sufficient enough to convince his Boss that he is the ideal candidate, the reality is that he did not meet any of the other necessary criteria to do so. Tom did not put time into building a cooperative and helpful relationship with his peers so he would not be considered valuable to the team and their success. And what about his overall contribution to the workplace? Remember we spoke about the difference between "Your job" and "The job". Sure he's good at his tasks but if his boss sees that he is not as inclined to do anything more, then his level of credibility with his boss will be less than he thinks.

Now let's take a look at Mary's chart.

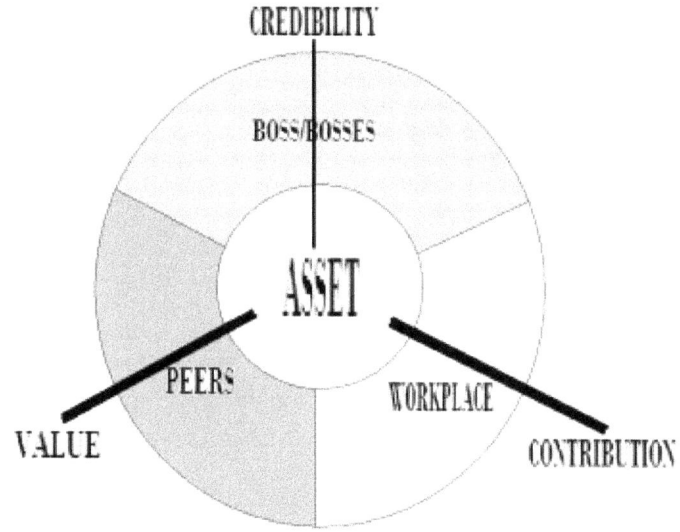

Mary's chart shows high levels of positive peer relations and substantial work contributions. This chart is particularly important because as a new employee this is where you would eventually want to be. And as mentioned before, this is how you develop credibility with your boss and coworkers. So as before, if the opinion of Mary's coworkers is taken into consideration then this will increase her credibility and potentially propel her to being a better fit for the position.

So this is Mary's final chart.

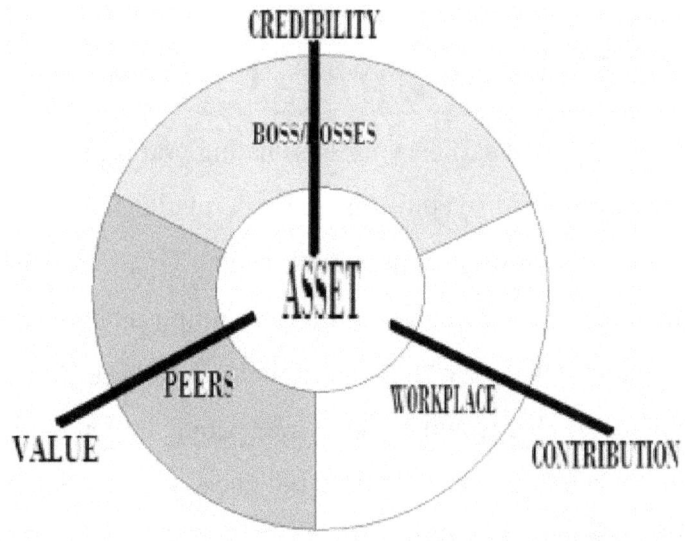

By developing positive work relationships and providing substantial contributions to the establishment, Mary has truly made herself a valuable member of the company. Or in other words, she is a true asset to the establishment. And this is the essence of being a valuable employee.

Developing a dual cooperative relationship with the people at your job and making an effort beyond your standard job requirements. This is the viewpoint that your coworker and bosses must have of you and your contribution to the establishment.

Getting Along With Your Boss- Boss Campaigning

As we discussed earlier, your boss hating you is probably a feeling drawn from a not so comfortable work relationship. And more than likely it's a matter of your boss not knowing you, rather than he or she does not like you. Although seemingly am impossible feat. Most bosses like to know that they know all of their employees. And why not? How can you be in-charge and not know the people in you organization. Most likely it's because your boss does not know you and that may be the reason for the uneasy feeling.

So how do you overcome such an obstacle? Well for starters do not wait for your boss to come to you as the solution. Because more than likely in their own way they already did, or will not, because you have to remember they have other things to do besides engage employees. So the next time you go to work you knock on the boss's door and you say hi. How is your day going mam? And if you're saying to yourself that's just crazy I can assure you that it's not. And that's exactly what you do or something similar. You break the ice. You take the initiative in sparking a conversation with your boss. You just may be surprised at how much conversation you missed. Who knows, you may have stumbled upon one of your greatest friendships or opportunity to excel.

Building a positive relationship with your boss is an important aspect of fostering a cooperative and productive work environment. If you want to move up in the establishment there is a tremendous possibility that your boss would have to recommend you for the position, and if the boss don't know you, then how could they. I have always had good relations with my boss as a mentally mature adult. And I say mentally mature adult because when I was mentally young and new to the work environment, I was a boss's worst nightmare. I had a very slick tongue and most of my responses would be cynical when being reprimanded by my boss. I took pride in my punishment and I think that made my boss even angrier.

I remember at a past job I was always assigned the worst post because you guessed it, I was the least favored employee. I worked this post for months and never made a formal complaint to anyone. One day we had a visit from our superintendent or my boss's boss and he was trying to find out how we were doing. This was the moment that I decided to bring forward my grievances. I informed my superintendent that I have been posted in the same location for months and never was told why I was never rotated. My boss stated that I never complained about it so he thought it was ok. I then asked my boss "if there was a possibility that I could have complained" then why was I always posted there? Furthermore, everyone knows it to be the punishment post. He then said again that I never complained. I then said, you never asked me if I was ok working there all the time when everyone else was rotated. He then asked, what's your point? I said, my point is that you show favoritism. He then said that he was the boss and he can post how he sees fit. So then I said, so you intentionally post me there.

The Superintendent had seen and heard enough of me sucking my boss into my conversation and tried to take over but it didn't end there. I kept dragging my boss deeper and deeper into my web, and he kept falling prey to my taunts. Now you may be wandering what this story has to do with the importance of developing a good relationship with your boss. Well let's finish up the story with the lesson involved. At the end of it all, my boss was liked by his other subordinates. I made him look bad and he even lost his cool to the point where the Superintendent, had to assert his authority to calm him down. I got my laugh and coincidentally was rotated at the other posts as the rest of the staff. But what did I really achieve except a few laughs from the crew and the infamous rebel respect.

A couple months later I was transferred to another location and I was branded the troublemaker. I had a good relationship with my new boss and everything was ok. And not because he was a better boss. But because I did not want to be known as a troublemaker anymore and I did not want to be transferred again. Now you may think that I should be happy working with a boss that I had a good relationship with but that's not all there is to it. My new work station put me out at least an hour more of travel time when my last location was very close to my home. My application to work in a different department was denied because my former boss had a say in it. My opportunity for advancement was gone because my former boss had a say in it. Basically everything I wanted to achieve or could have been was in the hands of someone who I showed I was not worthy to receive or become. And it became very difficult for me to advance so eventually, I had to move on.

So in my adult minded work experience I learned the importance of developing a positive work relationship with my boss. Yeah, I had my moment in the sun where I felt untouchable. Like I was the king of the mountain and had arisen to the position and title of full office bad ass. But that was all there was to it. Just a feeling. But since then, I have grown up and learned that it's better to make friends than enemies. And there is nothing wrong with me making the initial step to break the ice. Especially in the case of bosses where they could potentially hold my future in their hands.

Getting Along With Coworkers-Peer Campaigning

If everyone likes you, you're doing something right. And relative to the fact that you will be interacting more with your peers than your bosses, the relationship you develop with your peers will help determine the work environment you create for yourself and your overall value to the establishment. Create a supportive, trustworthy, peaceful relationship with your peers and more than likely you will work in an environment that fosters co-operation and respect. Develop a relationship that is disruptive and deceptive, and you will ultimately find yourself alone and unsupported. Although it may seem an obvious choice, it is a challenging task to create a work environment that is serene and will require you to work at it.

The basis of working with your peers and developing positive work relationships is built on the same principles of building relationships with just about anyone else. You will get from it what you put into it right? But we all know that it does not always work out that way so it may be necessary to take a structured approach to developing relationships with your peers. And for the sake of clarity, we will make a distinction between work relationship and work related friendship. Where the work relationship pertains to simply working alongside a fellow coworker or a group of people. And work friendship, relates to a friendship beyond the functions and interactions associated with the job.

So how do you go about building positive work relationships? You do so by establishing the three most important components of a positive work relationship. Now you can argue that there are more than three essential components necessary to foster positive work relationships but you would probably have to write a book to cover all of them. What we will cover is what I have come to realize are the three most important components and they are; support, respect and appreciation. So why these three components? The reason is that the work environment is not specific to one person and you will not be able to develop the same relationship with everyone. More so, the relationship at the job is not as casual as that of a friendship or shouldn't be, at least in the early stages. And in knowing this, you must strive to maintain a high level of professionalism with your coworkers.

But the notion of, you will get from it what you put into it isn't that farfetched. And to make sense of the notion: if the three components of support, respect and appreciation are returned to you, it makes it easier to develop positive work relationships. Supporting your peers is one aspect of creating a positive work environment that you will have to portray and will appreciate when it is returned to you. Although tasks and assignments are expected to be completed in a similar way and appropriate time, not everyone may be able to complete them in the way that you can. And who is to say that you can complete your tasks and assignments in the manner and timeframe that the company desires. This is where mutual peer support benefit's all. Support is simply what it is, help. We all will need help at some time during the performance of our tasks and it would be a good thing to know that we put it out there, and in turn, it can come back to us.

So what kind of support are we talking about? Is it giving support in any way you can? Absolutely not! And there is a very important reason for this. Our support should be along the lines of work and productivity and the overall benefit of the team, and not so much the individual. And remember this because support does not always improve an individual' work capabilities or performance. Now I'm not saying that if you see a coworker struggling with a task and you know they are making an effort, that you should not help them. By all means do so. But in some instances, people use the sympathy of others as a means of diverting responsibility of their work obligations. What you will have to look out for are the ones who pretend to be helpless, so they can have others do their tasks for them. And you should always evaluate if your good intentions are for the best or are you just being used.

The best way to evaluate the support that you give to your peers is to apply the principle of what "will it cost me to help you". And cost refers to more than a monetary aspect of support. And I hope that you did not already find yourself in a situation that involves you giving money to a coworker. And if you ask why not, it's simply not a smart thing to do and besides, if you have money to give or loan send it my way. The only financial exchange that should be of concern to you is your paycheck. Monetary transactions, no matter how it's transacted, usually end up sour so refrain from doing so at all cost. Support can also take the form of being ethical and unethical and in turn, be positive and negative. Unlike negative material and physical support, unethical support can sometimes go unaware to the individual involved in the negative transaction.

For example, gossip is one of the most common unethical practices that a new employee can quickly find themselves involved in. And although you may think that by only listening it may provide you amenity, you may be considered just as involved as the person doing the gossiping. So the best advice is to not be involved, have nothing to say and leave the conversation as soon as possible. Other significant costs associated with wrongful support can include job-loss, demotion, being overworked and even up to imprisonment depending on how far you are willing to go. So to be in the safe zone, evaluate the cost if any associated with helping your peers before you render your assistance.

But just when you thought thing couldn't get worst I have a bummer for you. Not only do you have to be wary of support, you have to support everyone. That's right, everyone. Remember, if everyone likes you you're doing something right. So even that really annoying person or the individual who takes a nonchalant approach to just about everything, yeah them too, everyone gets your support. Taking an inclusive approach to dealing with your peers will not only be a strategic one, it will also promote you as being unbiased and impartial. And remember, being impartial, unbiased and interacting inclusively is not a performance; it has to be part of your characteristic and belief. Now I know it can be very challenging to support disagreeable individuals, and especially those who do not share our work ethics. But in order to be a true professional, we have to do so. And by doing so, we contribute to the overall professional conduct and advancement of the staff.

The second component of fostering a positive work relation is respect. Respect not only shows consideration and tolerance for others, it also validates your sense of professionalism and proper mannerism. But being respectful in a professional environment is a characteristic that has changed over the years. Because of societal change, the traditional view of respect and courtesy is no longer a requisite for professional conduct. And by traditional view, I am referring to instances such as the once popular title announced before the name and the bonding of palms when we meet. But don't feel like you're doing something wrong or doing something that can be labeled as disrespectful. It has just become the norm to communicate and work in an easygoing manner in the workplace setting. And as a matter of fact, most of your peers and bosses would prefer to be called by their first name anyhow, without the pre words of Mr. or miss. However, a decrease of courtesy and respect is a common consequence of applying a solely casual approach to communicating and functioning in the workplace. To counteract this situation, a traditional approach to respect and courtesy in the work place can reinforce a mutual level of respect between you, your peers and bosses. But does that mean you take a mechanical and traditionally aggressive approach to communicating and working? Of course not. Remember people should like you where you work and part of doing so, is helping to create a pleasant work environment. So what you do is you develop a dual approach of formal and traditional work ethics and communication skills. With this approach, you will be able to integrate with your peers and maintain a high level of dual respect. And remember there are jobs that require us to maintain the highest level of professionalism when communicating such as a phone receptionist, help desk or any other job where you deal directly with clients and customers.

And the company may not take lightly to you speaking to the customer or client in any other way but a professional manner. So it may be a good idea to start practicing your sir's, mam's, misters and misses now, so you are already accustomed to doing so.

Finally we come to appreciation for your peers and their contributions to the team and the establishment. In many known public surveys, the results have shown that the number one concern of employees has been a feeling of not being appreciated. And just when you taught it would probably be money or job security. Now don't get me wrong. These are valid concerns that an employee would have but it just goes to show how much a mere thank you, can weight in the mind of an employee. Acknowledgement of an individual's contribution motivates them to do more and to do better. And I'm sure it does the same for you. In environments where there is little or no form of appreciation for work done, there is usually low levels of morale. Employees' with low morale will ultimately give low levels of productivity. So to relate your reason for showing appreciation to the result of it not being shown; if you do not show appreciation for the help and guidance you receive, your peers may not be inclined to give it to you again. So whenever someone helps you, be appreciative and say thank you. Just those two words can do so much for the individual and in turn, do more for you in the long run. If you do not shown appreciation, and it does not matter if it's the most insignificant thing they could help you solve (like for example, directions to the restroom); chances are, this negative experience could be the last time you ever receive their assistance. So those two little words can sure go a long way and more importantly, it costs you nothing to say it.

As we recap the role of the new employee, please remember the most important aspect of creating positive relationships with your peers. Support, respect and appreciation. Learn and apply these three essential components of positive work relationships towards your goal of fitting in well with your coworkers.

Teacher's Pet

Sometimes you can develop such a wonderful relationship with our boss that it can become an issue for some of your coworkers. And for this you can be seen as a teacher's pet or other crude descriptions such as a suck up or a kiss ass to be as direct as possible. But is this a bad thing? And should you try to remove such a stigmatism from yourself?

Well it all depends on the individual and what he or she can deal with, and hopefully its simply being able to see it for what it is. That its childish behavior on behalf of your coworkers. Some individuals can hear such remarks and pay no mind to it. They hear it and dismiss it right away. Others can really be taken back by such remarks and give in to the pressure. They eventually start minimizing their relationship with their boss in an effort to remove the stigmatism. And I think that this is the worst way to deal with this kind of situation. A good relationship with your boss is a wonderful thing and to give it up on account of someone's warped rationality is just absurd. Especially if it comes natural and you didn't even have to put any effort into building a good relationship with your boss. You clicked immediately. That's awesome. You accomplished something that some people had to work at and you want to give it up because someone else has a problem with it. And when you get to the bottom of their belief of you being a teacher's pet, it's actually their own fears of socializing with their boss that rules their rational. So in actuality, you have something that they want and you're someone they wish they can be like you. So the worst thing you could do is to abandon a good relationship to appease someone. And if you did, it

181

would definitely be one of the most foolish things you can do in your career.

Whenever you are faced with such a situation, evaluate the good before the bad and see where the real benefit lies. And this brings up a very interesting conversation. What good can come from being known as a teacher's pet? Well it's right in front of you. Someone is telling you that you have a good relationship with your boss. You can't be a teacher's pet if you don't have good communication, good rapport and proven dependability. I'm almost certain that as a teacher's pet your communication with your boss happens often and is very open and informal. You do not feel the burden of the employee-boss structured relationship and someone is telling you that this is not a good thing? Well good luck in all of your endeavors if you believe that their type of advice is good advice. As a manager, I have had good relationships with employees that went south because they were not able to constructively deal with the pressure from their coworkers. When asked, they would have reasons such as they were told to "never trust management", or "management will only use you for what they want", or "they won't have your back if you do something wrong". And I would say to the person ok, have I ever done anything to make you feel you should not trust me for which they would reply no. And then I may say hey, I do ask of you more than others and it's because you are very dependable and I know I can count on you. Is there something wrong with that? And they would also reply no. And when it comes to having your back, you're a good employee who does everything correct. I don't think you need me to have your back when your performance says you are just fine and can do it on your own. I then tell them that everything they heard from that individual was based on their own fears and poor experiences and had nothing to do with you and me, and the friendship we developed. And in fact, I truly appreciate you and what you do for me and the institution. At the end of our conversation, they realize that our friendship is a good thing and soon after we are back on track.

Now there are times when an individual can receive a name of teachers pet and probably deserve being called so. And no it's not me being hypocritical. It's just those situations where an individual makes their friendship with their boss so known, that it can be very annoying. This is the individual who talks about the boss and how cool they are. Or the extra perks they receive from the boss. Or the level of open conversation that they can have with the boss that most others don't. Yeah, that could get really annoying after a while so it may be best to minimize this kind of conversation about your boss with your coworkers. Although you may mean no harm, to the other person it could seem like you're rubbing it in. And if they have had a not so good relationship with the boss, then this will obviously make it worse and possibly create some sense of favoritism. So try to minimize your conversations about how great your relationships is with your boss unless you are absolutely certain that it will be beneficial to the listener if you do so.

Now being the teacher's pet can be great but it can have some negative impacts if you are not proactive in creating a healthy balance when it comes to a relationship with your boss. As we mentioned earlier, being a dependable person can be a good and rewarding attribute but left unchecked, you can find yourself being heavily leaned on. And it's totally within the territory because when a boss finds a champion, that individual that they can call on, they will call. And they may lean on you to the point where you feel like you are the only one working in the company. When you get to this point, it can be difficult at least from all appearances, for you to ever give less. So this is why it will be important for you to set your limits with what you can do early in your relationship, so that request can be realistic and doable. And you do not feel overwhelmed. Knowing when to tell the boss no is equally as important as telling the boss yes; but it's better when this is known early in the relationship as to your availability and usability, so you don't have to say no or the effects of no will not be as personal. As a manager, when my champion said no it would hurt. Even when I said it was ok, I felt like my go to operative abandoned me. And it was not because I was unrealistic, but because I always heard yes and had already worked the individual into my plan before I got an answer. If the individual had given me some insight that there would be limits to my requests, then I would have factored in the possibility of not being able to use the individual. And even if you didn't do it before, you can do it now. Because it's much better to keep your level of dependability, than to lose it because you are overwhelmed.

So what about your coworkers and they having a problem with you being a teacher's pet? How do you deal with it? Well it's not as simple as just let it go or don't take things personal, because your relationship with your peers is part of the fabric of a positive relationship in the work environment. So first and foremost, stop talking about your wonderful relationship with your boss and don't make it obvious. If you're doing extra work or an additional task, they don't need to know that it's for the boss. But you must also try not to make it so secretive that if you get caught it can appear that you and the boss is up to something. The less you mention boss in your conversations, the better it will be. Maintain a neutral outlook. Don't make it seem like you can only spend time communicating with the boss and you spend more time in the bosses office than at your desk. Don't make your perks obvious. If you get some extra time off or a reward you don't have to broadcast it. Disseminate a different message about the relationship you have with your boss. Are you trying to be a teacher's pet? No you're not, what you're trying to do is give a hundred and ten percent to the company because you believe in going beyond just the completion of your task, to ensure that the institution delivers on its promise to its customers and clients. And it would be nice to know that if you ever get to the position of supervisor, you too will have someone you can depend on and who has the best interest of the company. My willingness to help is based on having an attitude towards the job that's conducive to productivity with a result that benefit's all. An answer like this would definitely ruffle some feathers but I think the will get the point.

In the end, it's better to keep the relationship that you have with your boss over a coworker, who disapproves of that relationship because of a feeling. Misery loves company and that means people who are in a bad situation, want others to be in the same situation with them. They have every opportunity to build a good relationship with their boss just like you do and if they feel that doing extra is a problem, then that's their belief. As a manager, I can tell you that employees who go above and beyond reap the most rewards and stand the best chance of moving up. Just doing your quota gets you nothing except your paycheck. So being a teacher's pet is not a bad thing. Once you know how to balance your interaction with your boss to avoid becoming overwhelmed, and your coworkers to avoid becoming an outcast, you are in a good position to excel in your endeavors.

I'm Just Passing Through – Do It The Right Way

So you have a goal and this job is simply a phase in your journey. That's great, and the opportunity for you to gain knowledge and experience in your field can be rewarding as well. But just as important as moving on, it's also important to move on in the right way.

We have all probably heard someone say, never go around burning bridges. And it means that where ever you pass through during your path to success, you should keep it accessible to you because you never know if and when you may need to take that path again. But often enough, people do not adhere to this belief and simply leave without cause for concern or repercussion due to an unsavory departure. It would be dishonest of me to say that I have always left a job in the appropriate manner or given the departure process the proper procedure it deserved. Also, not saying that I just didn't care about how I departed, but the fact remains that I did not move on in the right way. And sure enough, my then actions did come back to haunt me. Not to the extreme of jeopardizing my opportunity to get the job I was interested in, but enough to have me worried over the situation.

This is why we must always try to ensure that we depart from any job in a respectful and honorable manner. Regardless of the type of job or the situation that led to our departure. Professional and procedural standards should always be the process of choice when we are in the process of moving on. And it matters not if it's a recent departure, or a job you did ten years ago. Your new employer can have stipulations that require disclosure of your employment history, going back to your very first job. Imagine being turned down from your dream job because of a dishonorable dismissal, from a former job you left almost ten years ago. I pose this question because that was the feeling I got when I was in a similar situation and one of my past departures was a concern to me. Never thought back then that I may regret not taking the time to make sure it was done correctly. And what if you're perceived move in an upward direction, end up being horizontal or descending. The grass is always greener on the other side and this is not meant to be a good thing if you have heard it before. And if you have had your fill of saying in this book, there's one more that your actions can bring you. Now you are stuck between a rock and a hard place. You left in a bad way and you have to stay and deal with what you got yourself into.

Now besides the probability of leaving your job in a poor manner and the negatives involved, there is one particular positive that I want to share with you. And that positive is networking. The people at your present job can have an influence in your future employment so it's always a good idea to maintain your network. Keeping in touch with past coworkers and bosses can come in handy at times and is a good resource to have. I myself have acquaintances from work related friendships for over 20 years. And the usefulness of these people in my network is priceless.

The true professional knows that he or she should always strive to depart in just as good a manner or even better one, than he or she came in. When you know you're on your way out, you put that much more effort into your standards and performance in order to leave that extra wonderful and longstanding impression on the people you worked with. The recommendation they give on your behalf could mean the difference in you getting the job, and not getting the job at all. And I can tell you that a great amount of consideration for a job can come from a recommendation or the manner in-which you departed the last one. And how exactly do you find out if you made a good impression on the people at your workplace? Well it's very easy to know if you have made that type of impression on your coworkers and bosses because all you have to do is ask. And trust me, they will tell you. Because the friendship you developed will be longstanding and continue beyond your encounter at work.

So when you decide that you are ready to move on, make sure that you are leaving the door unlocked behind you, because you never know when you may have to re-enter. Be as impressive leaving on your last day as you did when you first sat down to be interviewed. Keep in touch with the folks and take away as much knowledge and experiences as you can with you. And finally, leave one thing. A positive lasting impression.

Who Really Benefit's From Your Work?

When you work for a company, there may come a time during your employment that you ask yourself, "why am I doing this, I don't get paid as much as my boss". Why should I work hard when everyone else is slacking? And it seems fair because it's not your company and the boss or owner should be the hardest working people there. They are the ones who stand to benefit the most right?

So far, we have discussed topics on who is the greatest beneficiary of your efforts and contribution, to which we have come to know that it's you. Sure the boss in all appearances seem to be the one that benefit's the most but you should not measure your output by this belief. Nor should you reduce your output because of this belief. You should see it for what it is. Simply a factor of your work environment and nothing to do with you or you doing your best. And why your best, because what you practice you make permanent and your results and the effort you put behind it, becomes your standard.

Being judgmental of your boss and his or her position, coupled with the belief that they are benefiting from your hard work does one thing. And that one thing is absolutely nothing at all. Just you being judgmental and gaining nothing. Who knows what the boss had to go through to build their company or get to the position where there at. Don't you think that there is a possibility that the boss at one time came up through the ranks to become the boss? Do you know their story every step of the way and their efforts behind their success? Well if you do not, then don't judge. It may be better to use that time to be admirable and try to learn something, rather than using it to be resentful and affecting your performance.

Everything that you do is part of the process for your future. I often see and hear people say that they were not on track and that's why things aren't working out for them. But now they are ready and willing to do what it takes to succeed. Well I have something to say about that. The road to your success did not start today. If you feel it did then that's ok because it's your life and your feeling, but in the end, it's still only a feeling. You may feel empowered and full of the drive to succeed but what makes today any different than the last four or five times in the past that you said today is the day. The truth is, THE DAY started when you were first able to understand your efforts, the results, and the outcomes related to success and failure. This could have started in school, or when you first started working. Or it could have started when you became independent and had to be responsible for yourself. No matter when you did, that was the start of your success story. And with that being said, know that today, right now; you are exactly where you should be on your road to success. I used to be one of those people who believe that today is the day that I start on my road to success. But I came to realize that yesterday was my today and there was nothing that prevented me from taking a positive approach to my success. The truth is that we have to stop using today as a start and see it as a continuation point. Knowing that we are further behind and start with extra effort. It will also do us well by removing all those distractions such as the boss should be doing more, or why should I do for the team when no one else is doing anything. Do what you have to do to be better at what you do and continue on your pathway to success. This is what your efforts and your contribution do for you. Keeps you focused and on your path to betterment and fulfillment. So always do your best especially when faced with obstacles or hindrances so you always stay on course, and on schedule to achieving success.

The benefit's you receive from doing your job to the best of your ability goes beyond a result that is simply beneficial to all. There is another benefit that the individual will receive that can be very helpful in his or her future success. And the benefit is you get to learn leadership. And how is this a benefit to you? Well it is a benefit because a major part of effective leadership involves teaching people how to follow. And you can't be a good leader if you never knew how to follow. You cannot expect to manage occurrences of insubordination or failure to follow directive if you yourself never learnt how to follow instructions. Or showed respect for the directive of others. If you never learnt the value of hard work, how can you expect to teach and encourage others on why they should do it and how they can do it? How will you be able to deal with an employee that feels that you as the boss do not make the same effort as him or her? Can you speak to others with conviction, or counsel them on how to work through their feelings of wasted effort and how they can overcome them? I can only imagine it would be easier to understand and deal with this situation if you, through you practical experience have been down this road before and overcame this obstacle.

This is why I always try to do my best. And although my best may not be as good as my last effort, it is still my best. I do it because I know that every effort I make prepares me for the next stage of my life and my career. Sure my efforts will benefit more than just me but that's a good thing. It gives me a high degree of personal satisfaction to know that my efforts not only build me, it also helps to build something else. So why should I ever decide to do less? And when you think about it, as you continue to do less, the institution and your peers will feel the impact but eventually it will start to affect you. As mentioned before, what you practice you make permanent and with enough time of you doing less, it will become your standard. Even if you say to yourself well, "it's this job and the next one I go to I will be back to doing my best". Sounds logical but for what's it worth I see it differently. What I see from your actions is when you encounter an obstacle or a negative experience you reciprocate with negative and poor performance. And if you remember, the grass is always greener on the other side. So if you get there and you encounter a similar or worse situation what will you do? Less than your best - again? And if practice makes permanent, well you know where this is going.

Your best is yours to keep my friend and anything less is an injustice to yourself. So always put your best foot forward and strive for excellence. Know that others will benefit and be happy in knowing that they do because you are that damn good! Doing your best and seeing the positive results of your contributions is the key to maintaining your focus and achieving your goals.

Happiness With Your Job Starts With Happiness With Yourself.

Anyone can say you should be happy at your job but is it that simple? Can you just go to work and be happy? I don't think I can. And for anyone who can do it please share your secret.

Happiness in your job is like happiness with any other aspect of your life. Your relationship with your spouse, kids friends etc., it's a work in progress. You have to put time and effort into making it right. There are times you may be informed that you need to improve or make changes in certain areas, in order for your relationship to work. And for the most part, you do your best to build a better relationship because you know what it means to you. Even if you feel like there is nothing left to hold on to, you give every bit of effort you have to make it work. And you do so, even when others advise or give their opinion on why you should not. This is your relationship, and you are the only one who will experience the benefit or loss of staying or moving on.

So ask yourself, why should your job be any different? Do you believe that your career of choice will simply be a joyful experience and you will not have to work at making it joyful? Well my friend, if that's what you think then you may be in for a surprise.

Your dream job can turn into a nightmare career in a heartbeat leaving you wondering if you made a mistake. And this type of situation can and does happen often. But as bad as it can get, the one thing you should never do is give up without trying to make it work. I can only imagine the nightmare reality you can face if knowing that your dream job was disappointing, and the fate that awaits you at a less desirable career. There was something about the job that attracted you to it and you should always channel your mental focus to that point in time of being eager to do the job. Don't focus on the negative experiences you're dealing with right now. It could simply be a phase that you're dealing with and things could change. Being optimistic and having a positive approach to dealing with the issues, will give you the support to deal with it, and the mental focus to find your solution.

Being able to overcome obstacles and not letting them overwhelm you will turn that negative around into a positive outlook. Yielding further satisfaction with your job and most important, yourself. And honestly, this is where true happiness with your job stems from. It stems from you being happy with yourself.

Happiness with yourself in the work environment is about acceptance of the facts that apply to you, your tasks, the people you work with and the institution. And here are some hard facts that you must accept if you would like to experience job satisfaction and happiness.

First fact is that you won't have all the answers, even if your position dictates that you should. The sooner you know this the sooner you will lift a major burden off of your chest. You will be able to think better, and not feel overwhelmed when things go wrong.

The second fact is you can make mistakes. And anyone who thinks they are mistake proof is living a mistake. But more important than the mistakes you make, are the results that follow. If you can show that you learned from your mistake and have made major improvement, it can be just as rewarding as never making a mistake at all. Drowning in your errors will only propel you towards your certain doom and separation from the institution. So take a mistake for what it is and learn from it, don't become a prisoner to its negative effects.

Third factor of you being happy in the workplace is speaking your mind when ever applicable. But always remember to adhere to the rules of proper communication and grievances practices. Keeping your opinions to yourself will only cause resentment to everything you're not contributing too. But be realistic and know that your ideas and opinions may not always be implemented or received well. But it's the truth and it's how you feel. That's what matters. Your responsibility to your boss and coworkers is not to tell them what they want to hear. It's to tell them your true opinion or feeling on a matter. What they decide to do with what you say is up to them. And the longer you wait the worse it can be when you finally reveal your true feelings on the matter, in an outburst of cooped up emotions. Its better when it's a controlled format and not an outburst and you can achieve this by not internalizing your true feeling, in an effort to please or appease someone. Both you and the other individual will only suffer as a consequence. You knowing that it's not how you feel and they believing something that is not true. I for sure would like to know that the people I work with are straightforward and honest with me.

The fourth fact is that you have to make an effort to be happy at work. If things aren't going well, YOU have to make an effort to make it better. It is not only the responsibility of your boss or coworkers to make you happy at your job and build good work relationships. You can take the initiative as well. Your happiness is in your hands and you will be the one to make it that way. And if everyone else is unhappy at work, try to be the light of happiness for others to follow. You do not have to conform and be unhappy just because others are.

The fifth fact is that home is home, and work is work. There is no balance or trying to balance the two. The only thing you can do is get the both of them in order to ensure that one does not affect the other. You don't have to take work home and home to work. Neither do you have to intertwine them. The two can exist separate of each other and work out just fine.

Now the list can go on and on. But the point here is that it's not about the job, it's about you. You are the key to make everything right or everything wrong about the job. And if the job is not for you, then continue your journey to where you need to be in your career. Don't stay being unhappy at your present job because you are fearful of the unknown. And if you decide that you're going to try and make it work then that's ok as well because it's never too late to try to regain happiness at the job you're in right now. You have a choice. And there's nothing stopping you. And it will only get better if when you take action.

Do You Have What It Takes To Survive In The Workplace?

So we have come to the end of the workplace survival guide. And as you can see, it's not as bad as the title implies. But you have some work to do. If a successful career is something you want, then you will have to work at it. And success will only come by your efforts and yours alone. Now don't get me wrong, you will meet people who will be just as interested in your success as you are. But don't expect anyone to want success for you more than you.

The information contained in this book has worked for me as well as others, and I know it can work for you as well. Because it's not specific to any type of job, you can apply it to any career field you choose. And that's what makes is great, it's usability in any career path. And it's not just the newbie who will benefit; it's anyone who has been struggling to find answers related to the work environment. So now that you are armed with the information to succeed, let's see where your aspirations can take you.

"There is no greater offense you can commit than the one you are unconscious of. Because you are unaware, its end can be uncertain and renders the victim powerless until you have gained consciousness".

Barry David

www.ingramcontent.com/pod-product-compliance
Lightning Source LLC
Chambersburg PA
CBHW051213170526
45166CB00005B/1871